Finding
Healing

Finding Healing

Adessa Holden

4One Ministries
www.4oneministries.org

Copyright © 2017 Adessa Holden

The author wishes to recognize Jamie Holden for his contribution to the text. As an integral part of 4One Ministries, Jamie has participated in numerous editorial sessions and has willingly shared his words during the creation of this work to advance God's kingdom.

All rights reserved. No portion of this book may be reproduced, stored in a retrieval system, or transmitted in any form or by any means—electronic, mechanical, photocopy, recording, scanning, or other—except for brief quotations in reviews or articles, without the prior written permission of the author.

Published by 4One Ministries, Inc.

Previously Published by Morning Joy Media.

All Scripture quotations, unless otherwise indicated, are taken from the Holy Bible, New International Version®, NIV®. Copyright ©1973, 1978, 1984, 2011 by Biblica, Inc.™ Used by permission of Zondervan. All rights reserved worldwide. www.zondervan.com The "NIV" and "New International Version" are trademarks registered in the United States Patent and Trademark Office by Biblica, Inc.™

Scripture quotations marked (MSG) are taken from THE MESSAGE, copyright © 1993, 1994, 1995, 1996, 2000, 2001, 2002 by Eugene H. Peterson. Used by permission of NavPress. All rights reserved. Represented by Tyndale House Publishers, Inc.

Scripture quotations marked (ESV) are from the ESV® Bible (The Holy Bible, English Standard Version®), copyright © 2001 by Crossway, a publishing ministry of Good News Publishers. Used by permission. All rights reserved.

Scripture quotations marked (NJKV) taken from the New King James Version®. Copyright © 1982 by Thomas Nelson. Used by permission. All rights reserved.

Scripture quotations marked (NLT) are taken from the Holy Bible, New Living Translation, copyright ©1996, 2004, 2007, 2013, 2015 by Tyndale House Founda-tion. Used by permission of Tyndale House Publishers, Inc., Carol Stream, Illinois 60188. All rights reserved.

Scripture verses marked KJV are from the King James Version of the Bible.

Design: Debbie Capeci

Subject Headings:

    1. Healing—Religious aspects—Christianity. 2. Christian life. 3. Christian women—Religious life. I. Title.

ISBN 978-0-9988492-5-6 (paperback)
ISBN 978-1-937107-66-6 (ebook)

Printed in the United States of America

I would like to thank my dad and my brother for allowing me to share our family's testimony so that others can experience the same healing and freedom we've been given.

Even though she's in heaven, I'll always be grateful to my mom for following Jesus even through the hardest times in life and mentoring Jamie and I along the way. Every life that is changed through our testimony is because of her love for Jesus and her perseverance.

I'd also like to thank my dear friend Angela for listening as I shared my heart, encouraging me to share our story, for all of the wisdom, advice and support while writing this book and over the past few years. Your friendship means so much to me. When I grow up I want to be like you!

Finally, I'd like to thank the team of women who prayed as this book was being written and who continue to pray for the women who read it. Each one of you is appreciated more than you'll ever know!

For those who read the book, know that we are praying for you. It's our hope that you will start your own journey to healing, freedom, and the amazing life God has planned for you.

Contents

༄ Introduction 9

PART 1: OUR TESTIMONY

Chapter 1 ༄ Perfect 19

Chapter 2 ༄ Knots 37

Chapter 3 ༄ Failure 53

Chapter 4 ༄ Secrets 67

Chapter 5 ༄ Abuse 85

Chapter 6 ༄ Lies 105

Chapter 7 ༄ Shame 115

Chapter 8 ༄ Finding Your Value 129

Chapter 9 ༄ Finding Your Identity as a Child of God 143

PART 2: JOURNEY TO HEALING

Chapter 10 ༄ Allowing the Holy Spirit Freedom to Work. 159

Cahpter 11 ༄ Spending Time with Jesus 173

Chapter 12 ༄ Soaking in God's Word 187

Chapter 13 ༄ Investing in Counseling 197

Chapter 14 ༄ Forgiveness 207

Chapter 15 ༄ Forgiving God 221

Chapter 16 ༄ Talking and Journaling 231

Chapter 17 ༄ Lifestyle Changes 237

Chapter 18 ༄ Perseverance 247

༄ Notes 253

Introduction

A thief is only there to steal and kill and destroy. I came so they can have real and eternal life, more and better life than they ever dreamed of (John 10:10, MSG).

It was a beautiful spring day—during the last week in May, to be exact. I was between my sophomore and junior year at Bible college, and working as a secretary for the Pennsylvania Department of International Trade over the summer to pay my tuition. On my first day at this job, I experienced a life-changing encounter with God.

My lunch hour was about to end, and I was walking back toward the office thinking, "Girl, you are looking good today." I was strutting down the street in a great dress, fancy shoes, and sunglasses with the attitude that I owned the world.

I don't know if I caught a pebble or a crack in the sidewalk, but within seconds I went from strutting down the street to sprawled out on the pavement.

Splat! I was a mess!

My pantyhose were torn. I was bleeding. I think my dress survived. My sunglasses fell off. I was crying and my mascara was running. (This was before I discovered waterproof mascara.) In five seconds or less I went from everything looking great to being a complete mess, sprawled out on the sidewalk. As I sat there crying, an entire year's worth of stress, pressure, heartache, and disappointment came pouring out as I said, *"Father God, I've fallen and I can't get up."*

Physically, I could get up—I only had a couple of scraped knees. But something broke inside my heart at that moment and I was confessing to God—**"I'm exhausted. I can't keep trying to hold together the image that everything's perfect anymore. I need your help."**

The truth was that it had been a very tough school year, not necessarily because of the academic pressures or my work schedule, but because I was putting too much pressure on myself to be "perfect." I wanted to be liked. I wanted people to approve of me, but deep inside I didn't feel good enough.

I went the extra mile to impress the right people, build up my resume, and make the right contacts. I adjusted my personality to fit in with my friends even when I really didn't fit.

Wanting to be married, I drove myself absolutely insane trying to convince the boy that I thought was "the one" that I was good enough to be his wife. (Today I'm repulsed at the thought of even typing those words.) In the process, I took every suggestion he gave for how I could "improve" myself, including working harder at school, pushing myself into more activities, being more outgoing, and even changing my appearance.

Even though I was in Bible college and I loved God with all of my heart, my life was not completely surrendered to

Introduction

him. Instead, I had fallen into the trap of searching for my significance in the approval of others, in a successful résumé, in other people's respect, and the possibility of a relationship with a man. Still, in spite of all that searching, I didn't come home from college that year feeling more significant. Instead, I came home feeling exhausted, worn out, beaten down, and broken.

Fortunately, I had a heavenly Father who said, "Enough is enough." Using a pebble that caught my shoe, he confronted me with the error of my ways and began to re-navigate my life back onto his plan.

That day I remember him speaking to my heart and saying, **"Will you follow me wherever I lead you, even if it isn't on the path you've laid out for yourself? Will you, like the twelve disciples, lay your nets aside and follow me without reserve?"**

"All of my plans? All of my goals? What exactly does that mean?"

After thinking about it the rest of the afternoon, that night I said, "Yes, wherever you lead, I'll follow."

On that day, my journey to healing began.

Later that summer this question was followed by another.

On yet another lunch break in the park the Holy Spirit asked, **"Do you want your dad's religion or your mom's personal relationship with me?"**

This time I knew exactly what the question meant.

When I was four years old, my mom became a born-again Christian. A neighbor invited her to church, and my mom went forward for the altar call. I remember her telling me that the altar was packed with between one hundred and two hundred people, but the speaker picked her out of the crowd, came over and placed his hands on her face and said, "Do you want to become a Christian?"

She said that in that moment she felt like someone loved her and wanted her for the first time in her life. She knew that God wanted her. If he wanted her, then she was going to be his for the rest of her life. From that moment on, my mom lived out of a sense of devotion and passionate love for God. Every aspect of her life was affected by her passion to do what God wanted and her love for him.

My dad, on the other hand, chose a different path. He went to church a few months after my mom got saved to "see what she got herself into." He went to the altar because a very large older gentleman told him to go and practically dragged him there. Even though I was very little, I remember how angry my dad was afterward. He hated that he was being forced into this life and he resented everything he had to give up.

Eventually, my dad did find something he liked about church. Because of his job, people at the church gave him a lot of respect. He ate it up. It filled the needs that were inside of him, so he became very religious. On the outside everything looked good, but inside he never made a real commitment to God or allowed God to change anything about him.

In the end, Dad had a good religious appearance and Mom was determined that our family would wholeheartedly follow God. It wasn't until I spent this summer in my dad's world that I realized how different their choices and their lives really were.

Because of my mom's true love for God, she lived her life with passion, vitality, and joy. As I spent time with my dad that summer, I realized how empty and meaningless his life was. He was a bitter, angry, miserable man. When it came

Introduction

time for me to choose which path I would take, I absolutely chose that I was going to live for my mom's God and not my dad's religion—no competition.

When I chose *"I want a personal relationship with you, like my mom's,"* nothing was ever the same again.

It was actually the beginning of the end . . .

. . . the end of trying to be perfect,

. . . the end of abuse,

. . . the end of secrets and lies,

. . . the end of being all tied up in knots,

. . . and the end of trying to find my value and self-worth in things that didn't fulfill.

It was also the beginning of my journey to healing, freedom, and the abundant life that Jesus had for me.

Back then, I had no idea what the next decade would hold or that the road to the abundant life I was promised would go right through some of the most painful areas of my existence. I didn't understand that before I could walk in healing and freedom I had to be healed and set free.

Yet I have no regrets. Beyond a shadow of a doubt I know that the best decision I ever made after the decision to accept Jesus as my personal Savior was to allow God to heal my past and make me into a new person.

To take away the lies. Take away my hurts and heartache. Heal false ideas. Help me see myself through his eyes.

I want people everywhere to share this testimony and experience the same healing and freedom for themselves.

That's why I'm sharing our family's testimony in this book, to help others know that there is a God who saves, delivers, and heals.

Please understand that I am not writing this book from a place of pain. In fact, that's the miracle of our testimony. As you'll see in reading through the first section, our family went through some really hard, painful things, and yet because of the healing power of Jesus, I can write and talk about these things with no pain or anger.

That's the testimony: that God can take the hardest places in your life—the things you never thought you'd overcome—and heal you and set you free so that you can use your story to help other people discover their own abundant life.

As you start your own journey, I believe this book will help. In the first section, you'll find our family's story divided into specific areas that the Holy Spirit helped us overcome. Each chapter contains a look at where we were, followed by some of the lessons we learned along the way. My hope is that if you, too, are struggling with these areas, these lessons will help you on your own journey to overcoming.

Of course, I know that we don't all have the same story. The things that my family and I struggled with may not be a part of your life. Whatever your issues may be, the path to healing is similar for all of us. God has laid out principles in his Word and given us spiritual disciplines that will lead to healing and freedom.

The second half of this book focuses on these tools. I like to say they are guideposts on the road to healing. While many of these principles are touched on in the "What We Learned" sections, in the back of the book we get really practical and discuss exactly how we used these tools to find healing and freedom in our lives.

The purpose of this book is to whet your appetite for the abundant life that is available to you and provide you with the tools to help you on your own journey to healing.

Honestly, I believe that a lot of people are in the same place as we were many years ago.

Introduction

You want the abundant life Jesus has for you—you want to be all he created you to be, and yet you find yourselves continually bogged down, trapped in the same things.

The message of this book is simple: You can be healed and overcome. You can walk in freedom. Through the power of the Holy Spirit and the work that Jesus did at the cross, you don't have to stay trapped in your pain and heartache. No person is doomed to repeat the cycles of their past.

The truth is that when Jesus died on the cross, he provided more than just forgiveness for your sins and the promise of eternity in heaven. Although these are amazing things, his sacrifice also made provision for healing and deliverance. That healing is more than just physical, but it includes the deepest, darkest wounds of your soul.

It is God's perfect will that you walk in healing and freedom.

Yet so many Christians today say a sinner's prayer, get involved in church, and add Christianity to their already busy "to-do" list without really taking advantage of all of the life-changing, life-saving benefits that are available to them. They're settling for half a life rather than fully living the abundant life Jesus can provide.

Some choose not to take the journey to healing that is required because they want to avoid the pain and sacrifice. This choice is just misguided. It's like saying you'd rather live with a broken arm than go through the pain of having it reset.

Trust me when I say that going through a little pain is so worth the end result of a lifetime of healing.

Others don't know that healing and freedom are available.
Some may not know how they can obtain it.
Yet, it is available to all.

Today, I'm excited for you because this can be your turning point.

You can choose as I did so many years ago to start your own journey to healing and freedom and start really living the abundant life Jesus has for you.

Are you ready? Let's get started.

Part 1:

Our Testimony

Chapter 1

Perfect

I remember it like it was yesterday. I was on winter retreat in the mountains of Pennsylvania with my youth group when, during an afternoon session, my friend and I were talking with the main speaker.

Trying to make conversation, he asked, "So tell me about your families."

At first I sat quietly as my friend told her story of a broken home, an unsaved father, and the difference that Jesus and the church were making in her life.

After she finished, the speaker turned to me and said, "What about you?"

Almost instinctively I answered **"Oh, I come from the perfect family—Mom and Dad are happily married, they are both Christians, and we don't really have any problems."**

It was the answer we always gave—the answer we'd been trained to give and for the most part that we believed—we were the perfect family. No problems here—have a nice day.

Of course, it wasn't true. It can never be true. No person or family is perfect.

However, looking back some twenty-plus years later, I can see that it was this unrealistic perfection that was the basis for all of our problems.

The truth is that we did not have a perfect life—but we did have a good life.

My mom and dad met in high school and married when they were twenty years old.

Four years later I was born, and our family was complete when my brother, Jamie, was born three years later.

We lived in a ranch-style home that my parents built at the base of a mountain in rural Pennsylvania.

My dad worked as an accountant for the State of Pennsylvania and had an income tax preparation business at night. My mom was a stay-at-home mom who was passionate about raising her children to live happy, healthy, normal lives.

My mom was twenty-nine years old when she became a Christian. Several months later my dad begrudgingly answered an altar call and we became a church-going family. We were very active in our local Pentecostal church. Because of his job as an accountant, my dad was almost immediately put into positions of leadership in the church.

In second grade, I transferred to the local Christian school and Jamie followed when he entered kindergarten. Although it took a lot of sacrifice, this was a top priority for our mom who made sure that we had this advantage.

One thing you need to know about our mom is that she had a deep devotion to Jesus. She loved him with all of her heart and was passionate about living for him and raising Jamie and I to live for him. From a very young age she taught us to pray and read the Bible, she led family devotions, helped us memorize Scripture, and taught us that there was nothing more important in life than loving and serving Jesus. One of the best gifts she gave us was that she taught us the difference between "religion" and having a personal relationship with Jesus. She taught us the importance of being honest with Jesus and letting him do whatever was necessary inside of your heart to make you become more like him.

Looking back, I truly believe that everything good that was in our lives was because of her commitment to Jesus and to raising Jamie and I to do the same.

Of course, our lives weren't all about spiritual things.

We also had many good, fun, happy memories. Mom loved being a mother and she loved spending time with us. When we weren't in school, we did everything together.

The three of us were tight. We'd help her cook, clean, and do whatever she was doing. When we were done, we'd swim in our above-ground pool, go for walks, play games, and watch television, read, or go on day trips in the car. We had wonderful Christmases filled with traditions, fantastic birthday parties (complete with homemade cakes), and fun vacations. Because of our mom, we grew up feeling safe, wanted, valued, and most importantly, loved. And all of this led to us having a really good life.

The problem was that *good* wasn't *good enough*. Ultimately, it was our dad's need for "perfect" that became the poison that would fill our lives with a lot of pain and ultimately tear his life apart.

Let me explain.

You see, what Mom didn't know when she met Dad was that he came into their relationship carrying a lot of emotional baggage. I'm not talking a small carry-on bag—I'm talking a truckload of issues.

Finding Healing

However, he didn't tell her about any of them. Instead, he presented himself, his family, and his entire life as being perfect.

He had no problems. He had no issues. He came from a family where they never fought, never disagreed, never raised their voice or had any problems at all. They were the perfect Beaver Cleaver family.

Of course, this wasn't true—no family is *that* perfect.

What was true was that Dad had a lot of pain in his heart and mind and a truckload full of issues that he needed God to heal and help him overcome. I'm not going to go into exactly what those issues were in this book because those are his stories for him to tell. Honestly, the exact details aren't important to our testimony—it's enough to know that he had many issues buried inside that he was not facing.

Instead, he chose to live in a mental state of unreality.

Rather than facing his truth, he created a pretend world where everything was perfect. It was only inside of this unrealistic, unfeeling, unnatural world where no one fought, no one yelled, no one got sick or had problems that he felt safe and in control.

> Because the problem with "perfect" is that it's impossible. It's unachievable. It's unreal.

As a young woman, Mom found Dad's presentation of a "normal, perfect" family appealing. Coming from a lot of pain in her own growing up years, she wanted a healthy, normal, happy family.

It wasn't until after they were married that she found out how demanding, controlling, and stressful "perfect" could be.

Chapter 1 ⁂ Perfect

Because the problem with *perfect* is that it's impossible. It's unachievable. It's unreal.

Human beings are imperfect creatures and life is filled with imperfections, problems, and challenges.

When the standard is *perfect* it becomes clear very quickly that no one is ever good enough—except of course, the person who is defining "Perfection." In our house, this was our dad.

I mean, why wouldn't it be?

He came from the perfect family—obviously, he was the only one who really knew what it took to achieve perfection.

Being that they were always very open and honest (and healthy) about sharing their feelings and their struggles, it was obvious that my mom's family was not perfect.

Because her dad passed away when she was young, my dad said she didn't understand how to live in a family unit with men. Hence, he became the authority on all things regarding how men think and feel and expect to be treated.

Because his family never fought or even disagreed or raised their voices, while Mom's family was known to have a passionate discussion filled with emotions before an issue was resolved, Dad became the authority on how to handle conflict, control emotions, and maintain control.

This became the pattern. He was always right, always controlled, always unemotional. This laid the foundation for all of the problems that were to follow as Dad set himself up as an expert and final authority on everything. We either buckled under the pressure to be and look perfect, or else suffered the abuse that resulted from disrupting his false ideas.

To be honest, this attitude only increased when our parents became Christians and Dad was introduced to the concept of the man being the head of the household and wives and children needing to submit. Playing right into his need to control everyone and everything, he used these verses like a hammer to maintain control and make all of us follow his direction for how things were supposed to be.

The problem was that he was living in an unrealistic world and the way he thought things should be wasn't even remotely normal.

In his world, it was wrong to have or express emotions.

All conflict was to be avoided.

Fights or disagreements were seen as abnormal, catastrophic events.

Women should be quiet, submissive, free of opinions, and serve men.

The head of the house was never to be questioned.

Financial accountability wasn't necessary. He controlled all the money and disbursed it as he saw fit.

When something broke or needed replacing, it was a crisis.

Sickness or illness was a disaster—an interruption in his easy-going, perfect world.

Holidays always had to be over the top and perfect.

Getting sick on a holiday was cataclysmic.

Problems were to be avoided at all costs.

No one was *ever* supposed to talk about problems outside of the house. What happened inside the house stayed in the house—there was no need for the world to see our dirty laundry.

If you were the one who caused a disruption in his euphoric environment, you were labeled as a *troublemaker*. Causing trouble was the ultimate sin. Those who "caused trouble" were immediately labeled.

For example, whenever Mom expressed an emotion, she was labeled "crazy." It was common to hear, *"You know how your mom is—she lets her emotions get out of control."*

When there would be a typical marital dispute, Dad would blame Mom for *"blowing things out of proportion— you know how she can be."*

If she wanted something that Dad didn't want to do, she was a "dreamer" who needed to hit reality.

Here are some other labels Mom was given:

- *Religious fanatic* (She was too passionate about following Jesus)
- *Overprotective* (Whenever she'd try to protect us from danger that Dad's unreality wouldn't believe existed)
- *Demanding* (When she wanted him to take on more responsibility)
- *Weak* (He'd say she had a low threshold of pain because she had physical issues).

Of course, Mom wasn't the only one being labeled. I was a troublemaker.

Always having thoughts and opinions, feelings, and dreams, my propensity to question the status quo and my adventurous spirit were more than Dad could handle. I was always saying the wrong thing, wanting too much, creating problems in his peaceful world.

Because I wasn't what he thought a daughter should be, I was told *"Why do you always cause so much trouble?"* and labeled rebellious, unsubmissive, a feminist (a very bad word at our house), and a problem. Far too often growing up I heard, *"'Des, if you don't change, no one will ever want to marry you. You just expect too much. Even Jesus couldn't live up to your expectations."*

Another big area in Dad's unrealistic world: there was no place for sickness. Not that it didn't happen—he just pretended it didn't exist so he didn't have to face the pain of it.

This was a huge problem because each of us had health issues.

Specifically, it was a problem because my father and brother were both born with a hereditary disorder called Charcot-Marie-Tooth Disease. This is a neurological disease that deforms the limbs.

My dad could not handle facing this disease in his life, or the fact that his son had this disease even worse than he did. He pretended it didn't exist, for him or my brother. The result was that he forced Jamie to do things that he couldn't physically do, resulting in a lot of painful damage—physical and emotional. This is just a small example of how health issues were a constant source of trouble to our "perfect world." Through it all, Dad labeled us as the problem, as the troublemakers.

The real problem with these labels was that we believed them.

We believed we were difficult.

We believed we were troublemakers.

We believed that if we just tried harder and ignored the pain and problems, we could achieve the goal of perfection.

It's heartbreaking to write it now, but I remember hearing my mom pray that God would either help her be a better wife or take her to heaven so that my dad could have the good wife he deserved.

Chapter 1 — Perfect

That was just wrong. The truth was that Mom was a great wife and mother—she gave it everything she had, yet because she wasn't perfect, for many years she lived with the guilt of everything she wasn't and the stress of trying to be all that my dad wanted her to be.

The truth is that trying to live up to an unrealistic perfection isn't just hard—it's impossible.

But when you're told over and over again that perfection is normal and everything else is abnormal and wrong, it plays with your mind and tells you that you'll never be good enough, never be normal, and that there's something deeply wrong with you.

And then eventually, you find yourself slowly moving into unreality—pretending everything is perfect so that you don't have to face the belief that you aren't enough. So that you can hide from the pain, and hopefully, if you can't see it, it will go away.

When you're asked a question you answer, "Everything is perfect" because that's what you're supposed to do. Yet, all the time, you know—something's wrong.

That's where we found ourselves in the early 1990s.

I was getting ready to head into college.

Jamie was finishing up high school.

From the outside, everything looked perfect, but we all knew it wasn't. Individually, we were blaming ourselves and each other, but no one knew exactly what the real problem was.

Thankfully, God knew and over the next few years he would bring everything to light.

Along the Way, Here's What We Learned

Nobody's perfect.

The problem with *perfect* is that it's impossible. We're all frail, fragile, desperately flawed creatures who are incapable of perfection.

The Bible makes it clear: **All have sinned and fall short of the glory of God** (Romans 3:23).

Only God is perfect—perfection is an impossibility for human beings.

Not only is it impossible for people to be perfect, but life is imperfect.

The Bible says that man's days are hard and full of trouble (Job 14:1).

The truth is that real life is messy. It's ugly. It's full of pain and problems, laughter and tears, excitement and disappointment, heartache, turmoil, hard work, sickness, and success. Like a roller coaster, the beauty—the abundance—is found in the ups and downs, the highs and lows, the tension and drama of the imperfect.

> *Like a roller coaster, the beauty—the abundance—is found in the ups and downs, the highs and lows, the tension and drama of the imperfect.*

Chapter 1 — Perfect

When Adam and Eve disobeyed God and sinned in the Garden of Eden, the idea of a perfect world was lost forever and a new normal was instituted.

In our fallen, imperfect world, heartache is normal.
Disappointment is normal.
Difficulties and challenges are normal.
Sickness is normal.
Grief and death are normal.
Disagreements are normal.
Conflict is normal.
Struggle is normal.

Because of sin, the idea of an earthly utopia is completely abnormal and impossible.

Choosing to believe anything else is choosing to live in unreality.

Sounds depressing doesn't it? Please, don't stop reading.

There is hope. Because of Jesus we have the hope of salvation and redemption.

As Romans 3:24 (MSG) goes on to say,

> **Since we've compiled this long and sorry record as sinners (both us and them) and proved that we are utterly incapable of living the glorious lives God wills for us, God did it for us. Out of sheer generosity he put us in right standing with himself. A pure gift. He got us out of the mess we're in and restored us to where he always wanted us to be. And he did it by means of Jesus Christ.**

The beautiful thing about the gift God has given us through Jesus at salvation is that it offers us more than just forgiveness of sins and the promise of eternity in heaven. This is just a portion of the gift. The complete gift is that that through Jesus' death on the cross, we are offered healing from our past, healing in our minds and emotions, and the opportunity to live a whole, healthy, abundant life in him while we're here on earth.

John 10:10: **"The thief comes only to steal and kill and destroy; I have come that they may have life, and have it to the full."**

The Message says it this way: **"I came so they can have real and eternal life, more and better life than they ever dreamed of."**

So how do we get that abundant life?

What we've learned on the course of our journey is that the road to the rich, satisfying life that Jesus has for us goes directly through the path of inner healing—allowing God to not just forgive your past, but actually clean up and heal the wounds of your past.

These wounds may be from things that happened to you or be the result of sinful choices that you made. However, as long as you continue carrying a truckload of garbage with you wherever you go, you cannot experience the abundant life that Jesus has for you.

Ultimately, that is the choice that stands before each one of us: Are we willing to go through the process of having God heal and change us so that we can accept God's offer of

We are offered healing from our past, healing in our minds and emotions, and the opportunity live a whole, healthy, abundant life in Jesus while we're here on earth.

abundant life, or will we reject his offer and stay the way we are?

The choice belongs to you.

Looking back on our lives, I can see that a lot of the pain our family went through could have been avoided if Dad would have followed Mom's example and allowed God to start healing the pain in his heart as soon as he said the sinner's prayer. Instead, he went to an altar, said a sinner's prayer, and got involved in the church; but he never really allowed God access to his heart and mind. He didn't want to go to hell and he liked the attention and acclaim he got at church, but he never really gave his heart to Jesus.

He wanted salvation, but he rejected the abundant life that God had to offer.

Rather than allowing God to heal his heart, he chose to maintain the stance that he was "perfect"—now even better because he was a Christian.

Because he rejected God's offer to heal his heart and make him into a new creation, he stayed trapped in his old ways.

It was very much like the parable Jesus told in Luke 7:36–50:

The story starts off with Simon, a Pharisee, inviting Jesus to dinner at his house and Jesus accepted. Since Simon invited Jesus to his house it was up to him to be hospitable toward Jesus. But this was not the case.

In that culture, it was the custom to greet guests with a kiss. Simon did not.

It was proper to wash their dirty feet. Simon did not.

Finding Healing

It was the right thing to anoint their head with oil. Simon did not.

He invited Jesus, but that was the extent of his wanting Jesus or making him feel at home or welcome in his home or in his life. He did not even do what was proper etiquette for a guest who entered his house at his invitation.

We see in Simon's actions and behavior that he is a very self-righteous man. He is arrogant, pompous, proud, and full of himself. He was rude and condescending toward Jesus. I'm not sure why he invited Jesus, because it was clear that he didn't think he needed Jesus or even that Jesus was worthy of simple respect.

While they were eating, a woman entered the room— rocking the world of the religious elite.

Simon could not believe his eyes as he saw the local harlot—the town prostitute— headed straight for Jesus.

Simon wanted to throw her out. How dare she have the audacity to enter his house! He knew how she lived. He knew all about her. He would never think of inviting someone like her. Instead, he waited to see what Jesus would do.

He was shocked when Jesus let her wash his feet.

What was Jesus thinking??

Simon was indignant. He couldn't believe what his eyes were seeing. He couldn't believe Jesus was allowing such a woman to get near him, let alone touch him.

He confronted Jesus with a haughty, **"If this man was the prophet I thought he was, he would have known what kind of woman this is who is falling all over him."**

Jesus' reply to Simon was simple:

Jesus said to him, "Simon, I have something to tell you."

"Oh? Tell me."

"Two men were in debt to a banker. One owed five hundred silver pieces, the other fifty. Neither of them could pay up, and so the banker canceled both debts. Which of the two would be more grateful?"

Simon answered, "I suppose the one who was forgiven the most."

"That's right," said Jesus. Then turning to the woman, but speaking to Simon, he said, "Do you see this woman? I came to your home; you provided no water for my feet, but she rained tears on my feet and dried them with her hair. You gave me no greeting, but from the time I arrived she hasn't quit kissing my feet. You provided nothing for freshening up, but she has soothed my feet with perfume. Impressive, isn't it? She was forgiven many, many sins, and so she is very, very grateful. If the forgiveness is minimal, the gratitude is minimal."

Then he spoke to her: "I forgive your sins."

That set the dinner guests talking behind his back: "Who does he think he is, forgiving sins!"

He ignored them and said to the woman, "Your faith has saved you. Go in peace" (Luke 36–50, MSG).

Ultimately, it is about the attitude of the heart.

I Peter 5:5 (NKJV) says **"God resists the proud, but gives grace to the humble."**

Ultimately, each one of us has the choice of whether we will approach our relationship with Jesus like Simon the Pharisee or like the woman who washed Jesus' feet.

Many come to Jesus and invite him to be part of their lives, just like Simon invited Jesus to dinner. Still, for whatever reasons, perhaps pride or a desire to hold on to the lives they enjoy, they don't really invite Jesus to have his proper place in their whole lives. They want salvation—they might even like church—but they don't need Jesus invading their territory and making any changes.

Like the Pharisees of centuries ago, these people look religious, but they are really just tied up in the chains of bondage and sin while at the same time binding others up in the same chains. This was, unfortunately, our Dad's choice, and the result was disastrous for him and his relationships.

The better choice for him to have made would have been to come to Jesus humbly and say, *"I'm a mess. I need you. I don't have anything together—in fact, my life is full of pain and I'm falling apart. Please forgive my sins and make me into a new person."*

This is the choice our mom made. As I said before, everything good that happened in our lives was the result of her choice to allow Jesus to work in her heart.

This includes the choices that both Jamie and I made when we came of age and the Holy Spirit confronted us individually with the question, **"Will you allow me to do what's necessary to heal your heart, untie your knots, and put you on the road to healing?"**

With that permission, God began our journey from brokenness to healing.

But it all started with the choice: Will you exchange the appearance of "perfect" for the reality of health, healing, and wholeness?

This is the choice that stands in front of each one of us.

Perhaps today you need to make your choice.

Will you let Jesus put you on the road to healing?

Even if it means destroying your image of "perfect"?

Even if it means confessing your sins, openly repenting, and seeking help for the things that you need to overcome?

What if it means exposing your secrets?

Changing your lifestyle?

Admitting that you don't have it all together and that you're in desperate need of Jesus' healing?

Health and freedom are available to all who ask; but the road to this life goes directly through the path to healing.

What will you choose?

Chapter 2

Knots

$\mathcal{I}$ hate knots!

It doesn't matter if it's Christmas tree lights, untangling a cord, or trying to get a knot out of a shoelace, the experience of trying to set things straight is frustrating. Depending on the size or strength of the knot, I'm often tempted to throw it across the room or give up rather than go through the effort. Seriously, I hate knots!

Of course, not all knots can be abandoned. Some knots—like the emotional and mental hurts in our lives—can't be thrown across a room and avoided. No, these knots go with us, keeping us from being the happy, healthy people God wants us to be and experiencing the exuberantly overflowing life he has for us.

Trust me when I say, we know what it's like to be all tied up in these knots.

You see, the thing about living with someone who demands perfection is that it is really, really, stressful.

Real life isn't perfect, and the stress that comes from always trying to be perfect, to never rock the boat, never have problems, and always live up to an unrealistic expectation will tie you up in knots in a hurry. In many cases, it will make you sick.

As I said in the last chapter, Dad was a very demanding man who wanted things the way he wanted them in every area. So there was a lot of stress on Mom to keep to a certain schedule; keep the house always looking spotless with things not sitting around; dinner had to be on the table when he walked through the door and it had to meet certain requirements. This wasn't just inside the house, but outside the house and in the area of his home office where people would come. He'd actually go so far as to leave lists of things to do while he was at work during the day and call throughout the day to make sure they were done.

Financially, we were always living under stress. Even though we can now see that he had a good salary and there should have been enough money to meet all of our needs, we were constantly afraid that we were poor and would lose the house to taxes, not be able to pay the mortgage, or run out of money. Of course, all of this was just his way of keeping control, but it added tremendous stress as Mom was always looking for ways to save money and was under constant pressure to make things last forever so that they wouldn't break.

Then there was the pressure to always be happy. Emotions, arguments, sadness, sickness, or anything negative was seen as a crisis. It was extremely difficult to live under the pressure to always be up, always be on, and avoid rocking the boat.

Naturally, because we are human, this didn't always happen. The "punishment" for these times was that things were blown completely out of proportion. The drama that ensued made sure that you knew to avoid these times again.

Chapter 2 ~ Knots

In the end the stress to never feel anything, never say the wrong thing, never break anything, want something, or not keep up the perfect image was almost unbearable. I honestly believe it contributed to some of the stress-related digestive problems that both my mom and I lived with. Yet in our house, stress reduction just wasn't possible.

From the age of thirteen on, this sickness became a painful part of my life. In a way, this only added more pressure because now both Mom and I had the stress of watching what we ate and when we ate it so that we wouldn't be sick and spoil whatever was going on at the time. Unfortunately, this wasn't completely possible to control so illnesses spoiled more than a few "perfect family fun times." Then the sick person had to deal with the blame of being the spoiler. More stress and pressure.

Of course, there were two sides to this coin.

On the one hand, it was a very painful disease that restricted life. The other side was that as long as my digestive issues were acting up, my dress size was down. That fact played right into all of my body issues.

Body issues were another knot that tied up the women in my family. Mom came into the marriage with this pressure, and Dad's issues with women and pornography only increased the pressure.

Even after they started going to church and Dad stopped looking at porn, it was still a struggle. Mom was always worried about staying attractive because Dad put a lot of emphasis on how she looked. Growing up in this environment, it was easy to inherit the pressure that your value was tied to your appearance. If you wanted someone to love you, you needed to stay skinny, sexy, and beautiful.

Being a normal teenage girl, I wanted to be loved. I wanted to have boys like me and to eventually grow up, get married, and have a family. Thus, my constant battle to always look and dress a certain way continued until I was in my twenties and God started untying these knots in my heart. Although it never ballooned into full anorexia or bulimia, the pull was always there to keep my weight down through sickness.

Even more, I was obsessed with my appearance, and like my mom, I was petrified that if something happened that made me ugly or unattractive, I would have no value and no one would want me. I remember, too often, crying hysterically when something was wrong with my appearance. The knot that "a woman's value comes from her attractiveness" was just so strong.

Of course, the biggest knot that needed to be untied in my life wasn't just about how women looked, but untwisting my dad's lies about what men wanted in a woman and even what God wanted in a woman.

Again, because of the pain in his heart, Dad had a lot of issues with women—I mean a lot. Again, these are his stories for him to tell, but the result was that he had some definite ideas about how he wanted the women in his life to be.

I was born the complete opposite of his ideas.

Whenever my dad and I butted heads because my type-A personality didn't fit into his definition of how a female should behave, I was called unsubmissive, rebellious, disrespectful, or unappreciative of how great he really was.

This pattern started when I was about seven years old. I had just transferred from public school to Christian school and I loved it! Right away, because of the different environment and the self-paced curriculum, I began showing a marked improvement academically. Not only were my grades very high, but I was moving through the work at an accelerated pace. Soon I was working at least two years ahead of my grade level and loving every minute of it.

Dad, of course, was not so thrilled. He felt very threatened. When I did well, he felt insecure.

His response was to assume I was cheating. He accused me of figuring out the system and moving through the work without learning. (This wasn't private; he also discussed it with my teachers.)

That pretty much set the tone of our relationship going forward.

The next ten years were basically a battle as I was being myself while Dad tried to squash my dreams, personality, and capabilities to fit into his definition of what a female should be. Of course, I was always wrong and he was always right.

Instead of being proud and encouraging me to keep up the good work, his insecurities arose. The more areas where I excelled, the more he became hypercritical of everything I did. It was as if he always had to point out that he was smarter by criticizing me.

When I became a teenager, he frequently told me I wanted too much out of life. He told me my standards were too high. Instead of supporting my dreams, he wanted to keep me in reality.

I couldn't do anything to please him.

My personality was too strong. I talked too much and too loudly.

One of his biggest arguments was that it wasn't God's will for a woman to want so much out of life. I needed to rein in my personality if I ever wanted to get married and fulfill my role as a godly wife and mother.

Eventually, Dad's attitude toward me left me with a lot of confused ideas.

Is this how God felt about women?

Did God really want women to squelch their personalities and capabilities to make men feel better?

Did all men feel the way my dad did?

By the time I graduated from college, these questions were tying me up in knots. To a point, I had lost myself, trying to be the kind of woman Dad said a man would want. I was basically a chameleon—being whatever people wanted me to be at the time.

Based on Dad's lies that there must be something wrong with me, I tried to contort my personality or abilities. I was trying to be what God wanted, what a man would want, what Dad said was right, and the whole time the original me was all locked up in a box while I was trying to be someone I wasn't. I wasn't happy and God wasn't pleased.

The knots had a strangle hold on my life that were keeping me from the freedom that Jesus promised.

Thankfully, the Holy Spirit had a plan to start undoing these knots one at a time. Over the next few years, he worked overtime to set Mom, Jamie, and me free from each entanglement that was keeping us from being the people we were created to be.

Along the Way, Here's What We Learned

It is never God's will for his people to be tied up in knots.

Whether the knots are from the labels that others put on you or the consequences of poor choices that you made in your past, God's will is that all men and women experience forgiveness, healing, and freedom in Jesus Christ.

It is for freedom that Christ has set us free. Stand firm, then, and do not let yourselves be burdened again by a yoke of slavery (Galatians 5:1).

So often we read this verse without really understanding the background to which it was written. Although there is debate among church historians as to exactly who the book of Galatians was written to on a geographical basis, the apostle Paul's audience is clear.

Paul was speaking to Gentile Christians who were struggling with Jews telling them that they needed to convert to Judaism and follow all of the laws of Moses in order to be "real" followers of Jesus. Even though Paul had initially preached a gospel of salvation by faith alone to the Gentiles, the Jewish Christians were now coming behind him and saying, *"Sorry—faith and obedience to Christ won't do it—you've also got to start obeying all of the laws and traditions of Moses that we've followed for years."* They were even going so far as telling the Gentile Christians that they needed to be circumcised!

Essentially, the Jewish Christians were tying the Gentile Christians up in knots.

The book of Galatians is Paul's response to this problem, saying, *"Hold on! What are you doing? Why are you letting yourself be tied up in the very knots that Jesus came to deliver the Jewish people from? Don't do it! This is not God's will."*

Instead, Paul explains to the Galatians what is required for God's approval:

- *Confession of your sin*
- *Accepting Christ's salvation by faith alone*
- *A willingness to follow God's commands by forsaking sin and allowing the fruit of the Spirit to be developed in your life.*

And that's all.

Not circumcision, not jumping through hoops of religious ceremonies and washing your hands thousands of times.

Clearly God is interested in matters of the heart.

When you grasp hold of that truth, the Holy Spirit can begin to untie your knots and help you walk in freedom.

Misery loves company.

You see, what we learned on our journey is that like the Jewish people centuries ago, people who live in bondage always want to tie other people up in knots.

In our situation, Dad lived in tremendous bondage from the pain and knots that controlled his life. Because all he knew was bondage, that's what he passed on to us.

Freedom came for Mom, Jamie, and me when the Holy Spirit started showing us what Paul showed the Galatians, *"It is not God's will for you to be all tied up in knots. These demands you're putting on yourselves aren't God's will, but they are just one man's twisted ideas from which he needs to be set free."*

Freedom is found in God's Word.

As we began spending time with Jesus, studying the Bible, and being influenced by godly people who said, **"No, this is wrong,"** our eyes began to open and the Holy Spirit could start the process of untying our knots.

The more Jamie studied the Bible and saw that God didn't define godly manhood as who could run the furthest race, kill the most deer, rule his house with an iron fist, marry the hottest woman, or make the most money, the more he was set free to be the man God created him to be.

As Mom and I studied the Bible, the Holy Spirit opened our eyes to see that God didn't place women in a role that was inferior to men or demand that they squelch all of their gifts and abilities in life. Rather, the Bible was actually very pro-woman. Throughout Scripture God used women to fight battles, bring deliverance, serve as prophetesses, a judge, and even evangelists. Rather than inhibiting women, Jesus allowed them to follow him, listen to his teaching, support him, and play a key role in the early church. He gave them freedom to be who God created them to be and do whatever he called them to do.

Another thing we learned along our journey is that God doesn't just love us because he's God and it's a requirement. No, God actually likes us.

He's wild, crazy in love with us.

Psalm 139:13–17 says,

For you created my inmost being; you knit me together in my mother's womb.

I praise you because I am fearfully and wonderfully made; your works are wonderful, I know that full well.

My frame was not hidden from you when I was made in the secret place, when I was woven together in the depths of the earth.

Your eyes saw my unformed body; All the days ordained for me were written in your book before one of them came to be.

How precious to me are your thoughts, God! How vast is the sum of them!

One of the greatest truths that helped me untie the knots in my life was that God liked me just the way I am—after all, he created me that way.

That meant that he liked the fact that I had an outgoing, adventurous, conquer-the-world personality. In this knowledge, I was finally able to find peace and rest in the fact that God was okay with me.

I didn't have to work so hard for approval because God already approved of me.

As I learned to rest in his approval, I learned to be myself and like myself. As the knots were untied, I learned that it was okay to be who God created me to be—a driven, ca-

> *I didn't have to work so hard for approval because God already approved of me. As I learned to rest in his approval, I learned to be myself and like myself.*

pable, funny, smart, opinionated woman of God who wants to make a difference in the world.

Embracing God's plan.

After the Holy Spirit untied some of my knots and helped me to love the woman God created me to be, the next thing he did was help me embrace what God wanted me to do.

This was a big knot!

You see, I know beyond a shadow of a doubt that God called me into full-time ministry when I was eight years old. I wanted nothing more than to live my life in service to him.

Yet, there was a problem—I was a female.

In Dad's world and in so much of the world I grew up in, women didn't minister. If they did, they were out of God's will, rebellious Jezebels causing problems in the church.

What they *could* do was marry a minister and serve alongside of him. Naturally, I assumed this would be the path my life would take. Only it didn't.

I believe that one of the reasons I struggled so much with being single after college was that there was a giant knot in my soul saying, "You can't minister if you're not married."

More than dealing with the issue that I hadn't found a husband, I was heartbroken that God no longer wanted to use me in ministry. How could he? I was a single woman and that was against his rules (as defined by my culture).

This was a huge knot that had to be untangled before I could be free to be who God called me to be.

Thankfully, the Holy Spirit was untying the knots in my heart, and as I spent time in prayer and the Bible, he began showing me that all the "rules" I'd grown up with regarding women in ministry were man-made, not God-made.

Scripture by scripture, he set me free, showing me examples of women God used to work in his kingdom.

One by one as those knots were untied, I saw the truth that it was more than just okay for me to follow my call to ministry—it was God's will. Once the knots were untied, I was able to follow God as he led me into being a full-time, ordained, single woman in ministry.

But it couldn't happen until the knots were untied in my heart and mind through the power of the Holy Spirit. This is just one example. Jamie could give others, and if Mom were still here she'd have her own stories. Yet the point is still the same: The more we learned truth from God's perspective and allowed *only him* to define who we should and should not be, the more each of us was able to experience freedom and the abundant life that God had for us.

> *The more we learned truth from God's perspective, the more we were able to experience freedom and the abundant life that God had for us.*

What about you?

Perhaps today, you, too, feel like you are tied up in knots.

You feel like your whole life is about being and doing and trying to please people or living up to a false image of who or what you should be. No matter how hard you try, deep inside you know that you'll never be enough, you'll never really be able to do enough or try hard enough to meet the expectations that others or you have set for yourself.

Chapter 2 — Knots

Today, I want to tell you that it is God's will that you be set free from all of the knots.

God's will is for you to walk in his freedom, be who he created you to be, live for his purpose, and fulfill his plan for your life.

Obviously, this freedom we are talking about doesn't give you the right to live in sin or rebellion to God's commands. That's not freedom at all—that's bondage to sin. Instead, it's the freedom to know that God loves you, he created you with a specific purpose in mind, and he wants you to be free to live out that purpose.

How do you begin experiencing that freedom?

Well, the first step is:

Confessing to God that you are tied up in knots and asking him to start the process of setting you free.

The first step is always admitting there is a problem. Ironically, this is the step that keeps so many people from experiencing freedom.

Looking back through healed eyes, we can see that all of the pain and knots Dad created in our lives was because he was all twisted and contorted in his own heart and mind. If he would have allowed God to begin the process of untying his knots, he would have experienced freedom. However, he chose to reject God's offer and pretend the knots didn't exist.

Thankfully, we made a different choice. Because we were willing to go through the heartache and pain, face the truth, and put the time and effort into allowing God to untie our knots, we were set free and we no longer live under that bondage. But it all starts with the choice—Do you want to be set free or do you want to live in knots?

Going back to the book of Galatians, we see that Paul presented his listeners with the same choice. He warned them of the pitfalls of converting to Judaism rather than choosing freedom in Christ, but ultimately, the choice was theirs.

It's the same way with all of us: ultimately, the choice is ours.

No pain, no gain.

That brings us to the question of **"Why would anyone not want to be free?"**

The answer is simple: Freedom doesn't happen magically. It takes work. Seeing the origin of the knots may be painful.

You may remember things that you wanted to suppress.

You'll have to look truth in the eye, even if it's ugly and messy and hurts.

Just like a surgeon opens a wound so that healing can come, sometimes we have to experience pain to experience emotional and spiritual healing.

Just like a surgeon opens a wound so that healing can come, sometimes we have to experience pain to experience emotional and spiritual healing. When you give God permission to untie the knots in your heart, you're giving him permission to do these things.

Another key component of untying the knots in your life is:

Making a personal commitment to learning truth.

You see, most of the knots we're tied up in are lies—false images of who or what we should be.

The only way to expose lies is to flood them with the light of truth.

This means committing to reading and studying the Bible so that you can learn God's way of thinking rather than the lies that have filled your mind.

It's also helpful to get into a healthy, Pentecostal, Bible-believing church where you hear the Word of God taught so that you can apply it to your life.

Other things that helped us were:

- *Reading books by Spirit-filled authors and learning more about the Bible*
- *Listening to Bible teaching in our free time*
- *Talking through issues with godly people who weren't bound in the same knots*
- *Keeping our hearts open to the Holy Spirit to use every means available to speak to our hearts and reveal truth.*

The final thing that is necessary on your journey to untie the knots in your heart and mind is:

Putting the truth you learn into practice.

This isn't just a mental or spiritual exercise—it's real life.

When God reveals to you an area of your life that needs to change—a new area where you can walk in freedom or truth—take steps in that direction right away.

For example, one big area where I struggled was the knot of blaming myself for everything. As the Holy Spirit began untying this knot and revealing truth, it wasn't enough to just have the mental knowledge that things weren't my fault.

No, I needed to take it a step further and stand up to the urge to constantly apologize just to keep the peace. It was an action I needed to take to follow through on what I learned.

Questions to Ponder

What knots are in your life that need to be untangled?

Are you willing to admit they exist and allow the Holy Spirit access to begin untying them?

What are some steps that you can take to start flooding your mind with truth?

Is the Holy Spirit speaking to you today about a practical way that you can start walking in truth and gaining your freedom?

Jesus came so that we might have life to the fullest. This includes being free from all of the knots and chains that want to hold us in bondage.

Freedom is available to everyone; do you want to start the journey to be free?

Chapter 3

Failure

*A*gain, it was May—two years after my beautiful day in the park where I'd totally committed my life to following Jesus, no matter what.

Only this day wasn't beautiful—it was cold and rainy. It fit perfectly the way I was feeling.

I remember waking up the day I graduated from college and thinking, *"I don't even want to get out of bed—this can't be happening."*

Yet it was.

The girl from the perfect family—the girl who'd been an overachiever all her life—the girl with the big dreams to change the world was graduating without a job lined up, without a husband or even a boyfriend, with no plans and no idea what to do.

It was day one of my life as a failure.

Trust me when I say that I never saw it coming.

Things were not turning out the way I planned.

On graduation day, I was a complete mess. On a day that should have been a celebration of successful achievement, all

Finding Healing

I felt was overwhelming failure, heartbreak, and disappointment with God.

I just kept thinking, *"How can this be happening to me?"*

It was a mixture of sadness and anger rolled into a giant, jumbled ball of emotions. When everyone stood to sing the old hymn "Great is Thy Faithfulness," I had to fight back the tears that were trying to blast through as my heart seemed to scream, *"This is faithfulness? All I feel is let down, disappointed, and hopeless."*

Let's be honest: I was angry.

Angry that God let things happen the way they did.

Angry with people who made bad choices, and mostly angry that my perfect plans had fallen apart. Rather than dealing with my feelings in a healthy way, I pushed them down and plowed full-speed ahead, letting the pain and anger build in my heart. (Not a good idea.)

How could God let this happen?

What could he possibly be thinking?

I had a plan for my life. I had goals. I probably even took the time to write them down, and I'm sure I must have given him a copy. Didn't he get the memo?

This was not the way things were supposed to turn out!

All right, let's get really vulnerable and admit that I was thinking thoughts like:

"This is not fair. I don't deserve this. I played by all the rules—I kept up my end of the bargain. Sure I wasn't perfect but I never did anything REALLY wrong."

I even compared myself to other people who hadn't kept God's rules as faithfully as I did (please understand those last few words were written with a roll of the eyes at my youthful self-righteous attitude) and asked God, *"Why are their lives* working out when they did this, this, and this? I didn't do any of those things and I get left behind."

I was so angry and so hurt (the two emotions are usually intertwined for me). Every ounce of emotion was being pointed directly at God saying, *"This is YOUR fault!"*

This went on for several weeks. Looking back, I feel so sorry for my family who had to live with me!

I refused to unpack and accept the situation.

I tried everything I could to get out of the situation.

God didn't move (which just made me angrier).

I was angry, disappointed, hurting, disillusioned, and having a serious identity crisis. I mean, if life wasn't going to follow my plan, who or what was I going to be?

Even more importantly, who did God want me to be? What did he want to do with my life? Did he even have a plan at all?

What about that day in the park? Did God forget? Did I not hear him?

It was along the way to finding the answers to these questions that I began my own personal journey to dealing with many of the hurts and pains in my heart and mind. Even though the next thing on my "to-do" list was finding a job or a husband so my life would make sense again, the next thing on God's "to-do" list was dealing with my past so that I could find my identity as his child.

The choice that he led me to next was, **"Are you willing to take a time out and overcome your past?"**

To be honest, my first question was: *"What past??"*

And I meant it. I sincerely didn't see that I had anything to deal with. Yet the pain in my heart was so strong and I wanted out of where I was so badly that I said, *"Yes! Do what you need to do!"*

After banging my head against a few too many brick walls, I finally caught on to the road that God wanted me to take and settled in for a time of repairs.

Along the Way, Here's What We Learned

Failure is not an end, it's a detour.

Okay, my plans didn't turn out the way I wanted. But it wasn't the end of my life. It was just a detour.

Two of my favorite men in the Bible are Moses and Joseph—both were men who had detours that looked like failures.

In the case of Moses, the failure was his fault. As we see in Exodus 2, he was banished from the palace into the wilderness because he killed a man.

Joseph, on the other hand, didn't do anything wrong. His detour was a God-designed plan to save the people of Israel and fulfill his purposes in Joseph's life.

Yet, if we could talk to these men, I'm sure they'd both say that there came a point where they felt like failures and honestly believed their lives were over. It was hopeless. They were lost and given up for dead with no chance of ever having a better life or achieving their God-given purpose.

To them and everyone around them, they'd failed. It. Was. Over.

Yet, in God's eyes it was just a detour.

It was part of their journey to becoming who he wanted them to be and fulfilling his purpose for their life.

Chapter 3 — Failure

As I was going on my own journey through Failure Road, I drew encouragement from the lives of these men and others like them. I hung on to the truth that just because it looked like I'd failed, and so many people were more than happy to rejoice over the fact that the perfect family had a failure, in God's eyes, it was just a detour.

I knew in my heart that God had led me home and he had to have a plan. Even though I couldn't see it and there were times when I gave up hope and decided, "Okay, this is how the rest of my life is going to be," time proved the truth that it was only a detour.

What I've learned is that whether we create our own failure or God leads us to it, if we allow him to work in our lives, he can turn any failure into a detour that will bring glory and honor to him.

Never waste a failure.

The determining factor in whether your failure is the end or just a detour is ultimately up to you.

You see, one of the things I've learned over the years is that there are two ways to approach a failure or a "time out."

You can sit back, be angry, pout, and essentially wait for God to move, or you can make the most of it.

Thanks to the counsel of my mom, I chose to make the most of it.

How do you do this?

1. Choose to spend time with Jesus and in the Word of God.

When I came home from college, I was like a starving man. My heart was broken and I was filled with confusion. Yet, I knew where I needed to go for answers. I needed Jesus.

During my years of "failure" I spent hours with Jesus and in his Word because I knew that I needed this more than anything else in my life. So I set aside specific amounts of time to spend in prayer and reading and studying God's Word. As I grew closer to Jesus, his Word changed me.

The truth is that time spent with Jesus or in the Bible is never wasted. It's always an investment. I get so frustrated when I'm talking to someone who is in a situation similar to mine and I ask, "Are you praying? Are you reading the Bible?" and they say, "No."

Why not?

This is a fundamental principle. I'll be honest and say that continuing to ignore these things may extend your own personal wilderness experience or it may give you a permanent wilderness residence.

> *If you will commit to pursuing prayer and God's Word, even if your circumstances don't change, you will change.*

I can also promise you this—if you will commit to pursuing prayer and God's Word—even if your circumstances don't change, *you* will change.

So make the most of this time and spend time with Jesus and God's Word.

2. Allow God to heal the issues in your heart.

Although I did not see it at the time, I can now look back and see that God ordained this time in my life for me to overcome the issues of my heart and be healed and delivered.

Still, it didn't magically happen.

I had to choose to spend hours alone with God, praying through the issues of my heart, remembering things I didn't want to remember.

Then came the choices to forgive my dad whether he was repentant or not.

I had to choose to study the Bible to learn new behavioral patterns that I could apply to my life.

As a family and individually, we spent a lot of time in counseling and working with a minister trained in spiritual deliverance. There were so many knots that needed to be untied from all the years of lying, deceit, and abuse.

We did a lot of talking, and individually, we all did a lot of journaling.

The healing and overcoming wasn't instantaneous by any means. It took a lot of work and honestly, constantly choosing over and over again that I would allow God to take me through this entire process of overcoming the past and setting me free.

Even though it was the hardest time in my life, I have absolutely no regrets that I chose to allow God to take this time and set me free from my past. Without a speck of doubt, it was one of the best choices I have ever made.

Why?

Because I couldn't become the woman God wanted me to be (actually I couldn't even be myself), or do any of the things he wanted me to do until the lies and abuse that were scrambling my heart and mind were healed.

Until I dealt with my past, I was broken. All I had to offer God or anyone else was my brokenness—a twisted, distorted version of the woman God had originally created. When I chose to agree with God and allowed him take me through the process of overcoming my past, God was able to heal my brokenness and replace it with wholeness and the opportunity to finally find my identity in him. That's when things really started to change.

3. Learn everything you can.

It's important to realize that even while all this was going in my spiritual life and the life of my family, we weren't just sitting around praying and singing hymns all day. I was also receiving an education in more practical areas.

You see, I came home to a mom who wasn't just passionate about God, but she was a very strong, capable woman who could do anything she put her mind to.

She wasn't going to have any of my princess mentality. Much like God's attitude, my mom believed that I was smarter, stronger, and more capable that I thought I was or even wanted to be, and she pushed me to learn more and try harder in every area.

From that point on, whatever she knew how to do, she taught me. When we came across something she couldn't do, we learned together.

My mom saw each task and every challenge presented to her in life as an adventure—an opportunity to learn and try something new. Whether it was a spiritual challenge or a home repair project, her attitude was always, *"Okay God, we've finished that adventure—What's next?"*

I remember sometimes thinking, "Are you serious?" But that was Mom—always up for her next adventure following God.

While she was mentoring me, she was determined to pass this attitude on to me. I have to say that over the course of the years, we had many adventures as our home began needing a lot of repairs. After bringing in a few contractors for

Chapter 3 ∞ Failure

estimates, we realized that our entire family would be doing much of the work ourselves.

You have to understand that until this time, I wasn't exactly into getting my hands dirty. I planned to marry well and hire someone to do this work. God had other plans.

I remember early on in this process someone gave me a word of prophecy. It included things like, *"I'll use you to minister to women."*

I was up for that!

"I've given you a voice to minister!"

Yeah! Cool!

Then it came to *"I've given you hands to work hard."*

What? Are you picking up some static? Hands that work hard weren't part of MY plans.

But they were in God's plans. At first, we started off with easy projects, painting and wallpapering. Then we took the paneling down in my bedroom with the intention of painting the walls. To our surprise, when we got into the project we found that when the paneling was originally hung, they drew red lines from the floor to the ceiling every time there was a stud. That's when we learned to drywall.

In time, the projects became more and more challenging. At one point, we converted our back porch into a laundry room for my mom. That's when I learned about framing, flooring, insulating, and siding.

One of the projects I'm proudest of happened when we were having mold issues in the bedrooms. Jamie and I removed the carpeting and all the subflooring down to just above the studs. Then we replaced the floors and covered the floors with laminate tile all in one day. I was so proud!

As God continued to allow our house to need repairs, I began to enjoy the challenges, and the sense of accomplishment that came from the finished product. I too began to look at life as an adventure and enjoy the ride.

We didn't just learn about home repairs; we learned how to properly manage money.

Jamie taught himself how to do video production and website design.

We both kept polishing our skills as writers and speakers.

Little did we know that we'd eventually use everything we were learning when God miraculously opened the door for us to enter into ministry. Even the practical domestic skills I learned became the basis for my original online ministry to women.

You see, nothing is ever wasted in God's kingdom. The more you learn, the more you are able to invest in God's kingdom. So during your time of failure don't just sit around waiting for it to be over—learn all you can.

> Nothing is ever wasted in God's kingdom. The more you learn, the more you are able to invest in God's kingdom.

Take classes. Learn a skill. Increase your abilities. Understand that God's plan for your life may look drastically different than anything you ever imagined and be prepared for anything!

4. Don't make stupid mistakes.

Have you ever thought about what would have happened if Joseph had slept with Potiphar's wife?

You know it was an option.

He could have become angry with God and thought, "This stinks. I was the good son and yet you let this happen to me? I'm just going to do whatever I want—I deserve it and living right doesn't pay anyway."

But let's be honest—Joseph would not have been the eventual leader of Egypt if he'd made this choice.

It's the same for us. Just because God allows a detour in our lives doesn't give us an excuse to fool around with sin. Instead, we need to walk CLOSER to God and lead a holier life.

I'll be honest and say that I've seen it happen too many times.

People say they are in one of God's "holding patterns" and yet they are living a life of sin.

Guess what?

Sin is not going to lead you to God's perfect will for your life; it's going to lead you away from it. You might be on a detour, but it's in the wrong direction. Choosing to sin will never lead you to the life God has for you.

During my own journey through failure, I was very committed to not just living as close to Jesus as possible but also overcoming and resisting sin's temptations.

Were there days when I wanted to chuck it all and just go have some fun?

Absolutely. But I didn't, because I was committed to following God's plan for my life whether I stayed in my wilderness forever or if he eventually opened the doors for ministry.

If you're going through a similar experience, I encourage you, do not do stupid things.

Don't choose the pleasures of sin for a season. It's not worth it. Instead, choose to obey God's Word and live a pure, holy life before him. Allow him the opportunity to work in your life. Don't close the door on your own possibilities.

Can I add one final thought?

Learn to enjoy your life.

I remember my mom telling me during this time in my life that I needed to relax and enjoy it. She said years later I'd look back on this time and remember the quiet, the peace, and the time alone with Jesus and actually miss it.

I thought she was crazy.

But she was right.

The truth is that this time in life is precious. It's a once-in-a-lifetime experience where life is kind of "on hold" while the God of the universe works on your heart.

> *Don't spend your days and nights wishing you were somewhere else, but make the most of today.*

It's also important that you enjoy the people who are in your life at this time. Don't spend your days and nights wishing you were somewhere else, but make the most of today. Trust me; it will be gone way too fast.

Looking back, I can see that the life I was dreading on graduation morning was actually a beautiful one.

Although the detour took me through humiliation, embarrassment, failure, and pain, it also filled my life with healing, deliverance, the love of my family, peace, and joy beyond anything I could ever imagine.

It was the exact road I needed to be on to take me where I needed to be.

The same is true for you if God leads you down this road.

Chapter 3 ❧ Failure

Don't resent it; instead, embrace it. Take full advantage of it and see what amazing things God has in store on the other side of your failure.

Chapter 4

Secrets

When I first started writing this chapter, I thought about calling it "Boom!" because that's exactly what happened early that Christmas morning—our perfect world exploded and we were faced with the reality that things were about to change.

It was the first Christmas after I graduated from college.

Even though it was becoming increasingly apparent that things were not perfect, there was still an unspoken mandatory understanding that we were supposed to have the perfect holiday. It was a tradition Dad carried on from his family—no matter what was happening in their lives, when it came to the holidays, you did what you had to do to make them picturesque.

Only this Christmas, the Holy Spirit had a completely different plan.

Looking back, the clock had started ticking the day before Christmas—maybe even months before.

As I said, by this point in our lives, it was becoming more and more evident that there were problems. With each passing year after my grandfather died, Dad became more and more sullen, depressed, withdrawn, and silent. Although

Finding Healing

we didn't understand it then, what we later found out was that losing his dad started jostling memories in his brain and rocking his world. Unable to deal with them, he kept trying to push them down, all the time becoming more and more angry and miserable.

He was also very angry at God because he felt like God wasn't answering his prayers—specifically regarding Mom's health. You see, for about five years Mom went through a very difficult early menopause that had a big impact on her physically. Even though she tried every medical and natural means available to help herself, during this time in life she just couldn't do all the things she did before. This meant added responsibility, adjustments, and pressure in Dad's life, which he did not appreciate.

Rather than trying to understand what was going on and helping Mom, he got angry.

When God didn't answer his prayer and magically heal her so that things could go back to the way they were, he became angry with God. In fact, whenever God didn't do what he wanted in any area of his life, he became more and more angry. By this Christmas, we were all aware that we were living with an angry, unhappy man.

Over the years, our family tried different things to try to help our dad. I remember he attended a Sunday School class to learn how to overcome depression; we bought him self-help books, sent him to counseling. He even went to the doctor to see if it was a medical issue. Thinking maybe he was tired because of lack of sleep from sleep apnea, he even had surgery. Yet nothing changed him. The issues were in his heart; we just didn't know or understand what was going on.

By the time this Christmas arrived, Mom was deeply interceding for God to do a miracle in their marriage. Again, it was still too soon to know what the problems were, but it was obvious there were problems and she wanted God to do a miracle and restore their relationship.

It was also apparent to everyone that what she really wanted for Christmas was for Dad to buy her an engagement ring (he never had) and show her that he wanted to try to make the marriage work. It was probably the worst-kept secret in the family that year. In the meantime, she saved every little bit of grocery money or spending money she was given to buy my dad a special gift.

On Christmas Eve, they exchanged gifts in private.

And then things got really quiet—I mean really quiet.

When they came out of their room, it was obvious that something bad had happened.

Yet, it was Christmas, so they had to keep up a happy, carefree, holiday front. Still, it was obvious that Mom was deeply upset, no matter how hard she tried to cover it up. Dad was awkward, sulky, and angry. Jamie and I had no idea what was going on.

The next morning we gathered around the Christmas tree and tried to open Christmas presents. It was probably around the third or fourth gift that everything just blew up. Suddenly there were emotions everywhere!

But it was Christmas—this didn't happen on Christmas!

Blowing apart the image of the perfect Christmas simply caused more emotions, and before long each of us was scattered to their respective corners of the house to recover and regroup. Although I'm not sure what Dad and Jamie were doing in their rooms, I know for sure that Mom and I were praying.

One thing I had learned over the past few months of being at home was that God was in control of this weird life

Finding Healing

situation. After the explosion of emotions, I remember going to my room, sitting on the floor, and seeking God's direction. It wasn't long before the Holy Spirit spoke clearly to my heart and said, *"This is not your mom's fault. There's a reason for her pain."*

You need to understand that up until this point we were all still living under Dad's belief that you shouldn't show emotions.

Don't cause problems. Don't stir up trouble.

And especially never, ever, EVER do it on holidays. Yet, in this moment, the Holy Spirit was changing the way we saw life and making it clear that Mom was not to blame and her emotions were totally justified.

Immediately after the Holy Spirit spoke this to me, I went looking for Mom and found her in Dad's home office. I wanted to offer her support and let her know that I was there for her, whatever had happened.

When I got there, I found that she, too, had been talking to Jesus and getting an answer.

As we've said before, Mom was a woman who lived very close to Jesus. She had a deep prayer life and the gift of prophecy. Often the Holy Spirit would speak words into her heart which she would write down in the form of a letter. As she was praying that morning the Holy Spirit gave her one of these words.

In the word, the Holy Spirit said that he had heard her prayers for a healed marriage. It also said that he knew that things were broken, but he also knew why they were broken. If both Mom and Dad were willing to put the work in and make the changes, then he would heal their marriage. However, it was absolutely contingent on them both being willing to go along with his plan.

Chapter 4 — Secrets

So this was the good news.

Still, there were other parts in the message that we didn't understand. There were references to the need for Dad to deal with the issues of his past and cryptic phrases about secrets being revealed, relationships being healed, and changes that Dad would have to make.

Being completely honest, I have to admit that while reading those phrases, Mom, Jamie, and I had absolutely no idea what the Holy Spirit meant. Dad didn't have issues in his heart. He didn't have problems from his past. What did all of this mean?

Puzzled, but thankful that the Holy Spirit saw our situation and had plans to intervene, our parents talked, we all talked, and then we went on with Christmas Day. No, it wasn't perfect—in fact, it was the end of perfect. But it was the beginning of a whole new life.

So what caused the explosion? Turns out that Dad did not buy an engagement ring. Instead, he wrapped up a block of wood in the shape of an engagement ring box and said that this represented how he felt about her.

Yeah, she had reason to be upset. Things were bad.

We just didn't know how bad until the secrets began pouring out over the next few weeks, and months, and years.

Soon Christmas was over and the new year began. This was about to be a year unlike any we'd ever been through before as God slowly started uncovering and revealing the plethora of secrets in Dad's life. Again, because these are his stories, I'm not going to share the details of how each secret was uncovered and what the secrets were. It is sufficient for you to know that over the course of the next few years we eventually found out that my Dad had been lying to my Mom from the first day they met.

Everything he told her about his family, his past, and even about himself was made up—a figment of the unrealistic world into which he retreated. Behind all of the lies were secrets which the Holy Spirit uncovered one by one.

Of course, Dad wasn't just keeping secrets from his past. He was also living a kind of double life throughout their marriage. Around us and the church, he was a good Christian, devoted father and husband. Behind the scenes, there was a whole other world of compromise, anger, and lies going on.

One of the biggest secrets uncovered was the secret abuse that was going on inside of our own home. This was an incredibly hard reality to face. Still, one by one, the Holy Spirit showed that each of us—Mom, Jamie, and I—were abused by Dad in different ways.

We will talk more about this in the next chapter, but for now what's important is that all of this was secret until the Holy Spirit started flooding our lives with truth. For a family that honestly believed they had it all together, these were some pretty tough secrets to uncover and face. Honestly, we were all shocked when we found out what the others were going through—and amazed at how we missed it.

Another big secret that was uncovered over the next few years was that Dad had a secret debt. Having complete control over the money, all he told Mom was that we had no debt but money was tight. Then one day the Holy Spirit uncovered the fact that over a ten-year period of time, he'd been running up a secret credit card debt that had now ballooned out of control. Although finding out about the debt was really hard and seemed like an insurmountable challenge, it was the ten-year secret that was devastating to Mom and their marriage.

As we said, these were just two of the secrets that came out over the span of ten years. Believe it or not, they

Chapter 4 — Secrets

were not the most painful—they are just the ones that we feel comfortable sharing. Still, as hard as every secret was to uncover and process, the real pain was that the secrets existed in the first place.

Until you've lived through something like this, you can't really understand how truly difficult it is to find out that someone you trusted, someone you lived with, believed in, and loved has a life filled with secrets.

You wonder, *"How did I miss it? How naïve am I?"*

You feel betrayed. Trust becomes impossible. You start looking at everyone with suspicion wondering, "What are you hiding?"

Then there are the consequences, because ultimately secrets come with a payment. So often we weren't just forced to find out a new truth, but we had to figure out how to cope with the obstacles that came with that truth.

And it's hard—you didn't make the mess, you didn't even know about it, and yet, you have to help clean it up.

The truth is that secrets are absolutely devastating. They ruin trust, destroy relationships, and kill reputations.

> *Secrets are absolutely devastating. They ruin trust, destroy relationships, and kill reputations.*

Finding out all of Dad's secrets was an incredibly hard process that took years. Thank God we were also discovering areas in the house that needed work at the time. I can't tell you how many rooms in our house were remodeled using the adrenaline that comes from emotional pain. Anger really helps you hammer a nail!

Yet as each secret was revealed, it was really our family that was being remodeled.

And it was a gift—because each secret revealed helped us untie one more knot in our hearts and minds.

Each one set us free from one more lie or chain of bondage.

Even though the process of learning each secret was incredibly painful, the revelations revealed the cancer that was poisoning our hearts and minds, keeping us from being the people God wanted us to be.

In the end, the Holy Spirit's promise to uncover truth on that Christmas morning was the best gift we ever received. It was the start of our miracle—the on-ramp on our road to healing. The beginning of the end of secrets.

Along the Way, Here's What We Learned

Secrets are deadly.

They kill relationships, reputations, and destroy lives. Looking back, I can see that all of the abuse and heartache that our family suffered was tied in one way or another to secrets.

I think that's why I take this topic so seriously and am so adamant whenever I see a friend or someone that I love tinkering around with secrets and lies in their lives. Because the truth is that no matter how harmless it may seem at first, in the end, secrets bring pain—not just in the life of the person keeping the secret, but it also affects all of the people in their life.

We see truth in the life of Achan, whose story is told in Joshua 7. From the very first time his name is mentioned in Scripture, we see that a person who keeps secrets doesn't just hurt themselves. Secrets spread a wide circle that hurts everyone around us.

> **But Israel violated the instructions about the things set apart for the Lord. A man named Achan had stolen some of these dedicated things, so the Lord was very angry with the Israelites. Achan was the son of Carmi, a descendant of Zimri son of Zerah, of the tribe of Judah** (Joshua 7:1, NLT).

I'm sure when Achan stole and hid the dedicated things he thought it was no big deal—his own little secret stash. Yet, notice that the Bible says that **"Israel sinned."** Ultimately, the whole country suffered because of one man's secrets.

Because God couldn't bless hidden sin, the entire country lost the battle.

More specifically, thirty-six men lost their lives and thirty-six families suffered grief.

In the end, when Achan's sin was discovered, he wasn't the only one punished. Instead, Achan and his entire family died and all of their possessions were burned when his sin was discovered (Joshua 7:24–26).

That's the sad thing about secrets: They don't just hurt one person. They touch the lives of everyone being deceived. As I look back on the pattern of secrets and lies in our family, the truth is that I don't know where they originated. All I can see is the trail of wounded lives they left behind.

Another truth we see in the life of Achan is that:

God already knows your secret.

I'm guessing that after Achan stole the devoted things, he thought he got away with it. With no one the wiser, he was home free.

The only problem is that God knew and he couldn't allow Achan's secret to remain hidden. He had to expose Achan's sin so that the Israelites could stop being defeated by their enemies and go into their Promised Land.

You see, God can't bless sin—yet God wants to bless us.

That's why he will try every means necessary to first get you to confess your sin and then if you still refuse, he will expose your sin and secrets. It's part of his kindness that leads to repentance.

Even though it may seem cruel at first, what we learned was that exposing secrets is actually the kindest thing God can do. Because it isn't until the secrets are brought into the light that they stop holding you and the people in your life in bondage.

Looking back, I'm grateful that God knew Dad's secrets and exposed them. Even though it was an excruciatingly hard time in life, once the secrets were out our lives changed dramatically for the better.

> *That's the sad thing about secrets: They don't just hurt one person. They touch the lives of everyone being deceived.*

Chapter 4 ✺ Secrets

What if you're caught in a web of lies?

Then it's time to repent. Come clean. Confess.

Start by asking God to forgive you for the sin of lying and deceit.

Then go to everyone you've been lying to and keeping secrets from and ask them to forgive you.

Honestly, this is the choice that we wish Dad would have made. Thinking back, the Holy Spirit certainly gave him enough opportunities—especially when it came time to confessing his secret debt.

It was about five days before what we'd later refer to as "D-Day."

Jamie was away at college. Dad, Mom, and I were shopping for a used car when my mom asked, "Do we have any other debt that we should pay off before we buy a car?"

All of a sudden my dad got very agitated and adamantly said, "Don't you believe me? I've told you over and over, we have no debt."

The overreaction seemed odd, but wanting to avoid his angry mood we dropped the issue and put off buying the car.

A few days later, my dad was in a counseling session when his counselor felt impressed by the Holy Spirit to ask several times, "Are you hiding something that you need to confess?"

Dad says he knew then he should have confessed the debt, but he chose not to say anything. The next day, Mom opened the mail and his secret debt was exposed.

This wasn't just the case with the debt. I remember months earlier Dad had received a note in the mail from a man in his men's group saying, "I've been praying for you and the Holy Spirit wanted me to tell you that there are things you need to confess to your wife and stop keeping secrets."

Again, rather than responding to the Holy Spirit's promptings, my dad became furious with the man and told the man to stop causing trouble in his marriage. Over and over again, the Holy Spirit tried to help Dad repent and change willingly, but because Dad ignored this grace, God had to expose his sin for the sake of the people it was hurting.

Today if you're reading this and you're trapped by secrets, please learn from our dad's life. Don't believe the lie that you'll never get caught. Remember that God knows the truth and because he loves you and the people your secrets are affecting, he will expose you.

But there is another option: You can come clean and reveal your own secrets.

I remember Mom saying, *"It would have been so much better if he (our dad) had confessed, but because he got caught, I'll never know if he was really sorry or if he can ever be trusted again."*

There's something about a person coming forward, taking responsibility for their actions and telling the truth that seems honorable . . . as if the person is truly sorry.

Getting caught is just getting caught.

So do the right thing—repent and confess.

Take responsibility for your mess and help clean it up.

Then vow to abandon lying and secrets forever and open yourself up to accountability.

Here's a tip: Don't expect it to be easy.

Even though confession is the right thing to do, it isn't easy.

Chapter 4 — Secrets

Don't expect it to be easy for you or or the people who are learning about your secrets.

First of all, they are going to be shocked. It's going to take time for them to wrap their minds around what is new information for them.

After the shock wears off they will probably be hurt and angry. They are going to have their own emotions that they'll need to work through.

Remember: you victimized them, so don't expect them to help you. Find an unbiased third party—preferably a counselor or a minister—to help you and allow the people you hurt to find people to help them.

Understand that it will be hard for people to trust you again, and devote yourself to re-establishing trust.

Remember—they don't owe trust to you and may never be able to fully give it to you again—be grateful that they are still trying and keep on the straight and narrow.

You may even suffer some consequences or need to make restitution. These are the consequences of secrets.

Still, as someone who has lived through this nightmare, I can tell you that it will be so much better if you confess than if you are exposed. Please listen to this warning and re-

> *As someone who has lived through this nightmare, I can tell you that it will be so much better if you confess than if you are exposed.*

alize that although no path to overcoming secrets is easy, it's so much harder if you get caught than if you confess.

Most importantly, don't blow this off.

If you are lying—keeping a secret from someone you love—don't make excuses and pretend it's no big deal.

Instead, realize that you are sinning against God.

Face the fact that you are playing with fire.

Heed the warning and turn around. Stop lying and start living a life of truth.

Make the wisest choice you can ever make: Come clean, confess your sins, and tell your own secrets and start living in truth today.

There is hope for those trapped in secrets, but it only comes through truth.

Therefore confess your sins to each other and pray for each other so that you may be healed (James 5:16).

The longer you keep your secrets, the more pain they are causing.

The more you lie, the harder it will be to regain trust.

Today if you are reading this chapter and you're caught up in secrets, do what is necessary to confess and start living in truth. Even though overcoming the pain of the past is hard, abandoning secrets is the first step to a better future.

There is hope for those trapped in secrets, but it only comes through truth.

Start pursuing truth today.

Then you will know the truth, and the truth will set you free (John 8:32).

How do you survive secrets?

What do you do if you are on the other side of the coin and are the victim of secrets?

You survive only through God. It is totally God who must give you the grace to forgive the person who hurt you so badly. It is God who must take the excruciating pain out of your soul as you talk to God and pour out your emotions.

Please don't think I'm making light of being the victim of secret living. I understand that it is devastating.

And the pain doesn't go away magically or instantly. It hurts and will hurt for a while. These are deep hurts that will absolutely take time and the healing of the Holy Spirit to overcome.

You may need counseling.

It's good to hear the perspective of a mature, Spirit-filled believer who isn't suffering from emotional pain to help you see things clearly. That kind of person will help you know what you should do next and what changes to make and expect going forward. We went to counseling individually and as a family to overcome the damage secrets did to our lives. It also helped us to learn new behavioral patterns.

Looking back, I honestly do not know how we would have survived without the pastor who provided counseling—making himself available when we needed it. Truthfully, we needed a lot of help.

If you're the victim of secrets I encourage you that, in addition to spending hours with God pouring out your heart to him and allowing him to heal you, you need to find a counselor. You need someone who will listen to your pain and help you decide where to go from here.

One thing is for sure:

When a secret is uncovered, it brings change.

It has to. You can't just pretend it didn't happen, sweep it under the carpet and go on as usual.

For example, when we found out about the secret abuse in our lives, we took steps to make sure that it ended.

When the secret debt was revealed, everything about our how money was handled in our family changed. When Dad couldn't have complete control, he left Mom with the burden of cleaning up his mess and getting our family back on track.

However: Here's an important truth:

Change is an opportunity to make things better.

Finding out about my dad's secret debt was devastating, but the changes that followed made our lives so much better. As Mom committed to learning God's financial principles and applying them to our lives, we were finally, for the first time ever, able to live life without being afraid of money.

We started living on a budget and loved it! Eventually, we paid off the debt and start saving. Most of all, we were no longer controlled by money or Dad.

With truth comes change. The change was hard but it shifted everything—for the better.

Another important key that we learned in our journey to living free from secrets is:

You need to stop keeping secrets.

I know it sounds obvious and redundant, but it's vitally important that you don't allow the fact that there are secrets to become a secret that ties you up in more knots.

Instead, you need to make the decision to kick secrets out of your life by talking.

Tell your story.

Share what you've been through and how God helped you through it.

The best way to break the chains of secrets is by sharing the secrets so that they can't control you anymore.

Looking back, we wish Dad would have made this decision so much earlier in his life. I'm sure he wishes he would have too because he would have had a much better life. However, that didn't happen and his secrets caused our family a lot of pain, and honestly, a lot of destruction.

> Don't allow the fact that there are secrets to become a secret that ties you up in more knots.

Thankfully, because of the redeeming power of Jesus, we were able to make another choice. After fighting through the shock, pain, betrayal, and effects these secrets had on our lives, we were able to overcome.

Today our lives are an open book—a testimony to God's faithfulness.

Our greatest secrets and shame have become a testimony that God can make beauty from ashes and that truth really does set people free.

This can be your testimony, too.

You don't have to stay bound in secrets.

You, too, can be free if you're willing to confess, repent, deal with the consequences, and start living in truth.

It's a hard road, but it's the only road to freedom.

Chapter 5

Abuse

We never really thought it would be part of our story. After all, we were perfect.

Besides that, we grew up in a Christian home, our family went to church, and we seemed to have it all together.

Especially Dad. The truth is that looking at our lives from the outside he was the last person you would ever expect to be an abuser.

He was always so calm and in control. It was almost eerie how much he controlled his emotions—never feeling much of anything or displaying any real emotion—and being deeply critical of anyone who did.

Yet, after that Christmas when the Holy Spirit intervened in our lives, things began to change. That's when abuse became a prominent part of our story.

Honestly, we had absolutely no idea what was going on.

You see, after the Holy Spirit spoke to our mom on Christmas Day, she wanted everything God offered—a new marriage, healing, deliverance—basically a chance to start fresh. We thought Dad wanted the same thing because he said he did. (We later realized that his pattern was to say whatever was necessary at the time to get people off his back, but we didn't know this then.)

Knowing the steps to healing, Mom started pursuing them.

She wanted to talk about issues and try to resolve them inside our family and with people who had been a source of pain in our family for years.

Dad was having none of it. Even though he agreed to go to counseling, he wouldn't stick with one counselor. Instead, every time a counselor would get near his issues, he'd say they were crazy and he needed to switch. This started the pattern of going to counselor after counselor, but never really getting any help.

Still, the pursuit of freedom was hitting a nerve in his mind and heart. The Holy Spirit was at work in the hearts of the rest of the family.

We were working through issues, trying to resolve problems inside and outside of the family, and secrets were starting to be uncovered. Combine this with the fact that the Holy Spirit was starting to uncover memories in his own mind that needed to be healed, and Dad's world was shaking. "Perfect" was being blown to pieces and harsh reality was coming to the surface.

Rather than surrendering fully to God and going through the painful process of remembering and healing, Dad chose to try to regain and retain control of the situation.

By the fall of 1997, Mom and I were living a nightmare. Jamie was away at college and Dad's "anger episodes" were becoming more and more common. They were also turning violent. I remember spending nights behind locked bedroom doors waiting for him to fall asleep, or go to work, or to calm down.

Chapter 5 ~ Abuse

We never knew what was going to set him off. After each episode, he was very remorseful and sorry, even a little shocked that it happened. Still, it didn't keep it from happening again.

It happened way too often. We had no idea what to do.

It was absolutely horrifying, but you could see it coming on.

It would start with a look in his eyes or a hardness he'd get around his face. It was almost as if his eyes would become black or there'd be a steely focus come over his pupils. The scariest part was how incredibly cold his eyes would become. It was like he'd look right through you with hate. His face would become hard and you knew wild behavior would soon follow.

Then "Boom!"

I remember one time Mom, Dad, and I were all sitting around the dining room table playing a game. The next day was her birthday and it was supposed to be a beautiful day. She brought up the idea that it would be nice to drive down to the beach for the day.

The next thing we knew Dad was having a violent temper tantrum. He was throwing things around, threatening to break the dining room chairs and acting like a crazy man. Finally, he went to his room and Mom and I just stayed together waiting for him to fall asleep, then get up and go to work.

We were shocked. Stunned. And honestly afraid.

I'm sad to say there were too many nights like that. We eventually started sleeping with baseball bats and rolling pins.

Another day, when Jamie was home from college, we'd all gone to church together and we were talking about what the minister said on the way home. Dad was driving and I guess he didn't like what was being said because all of a sudden he started driving erratically and swerving as if he was going to drive off the side of the mountain.

The conversation changed real fast as his tactics allowed him to regain control!

Looking back now, we can see that this was always the reason for the temper tantrums, the violence, or the abuse—he used fear to gain control. Although this is not true in every case, there was a demonic element influencing or even controlling Dad at this time.

Now I know this is controversial and many people will say that this isn't possible because a Christian can't have a demon. My answer is simply that I do not believe Dad was a Christian at this point in his life.

True, he had said a sinner's prayer years earlier and he still called himself a Christian, but he was also living in complete disobedience and rebellion to God. His whole life was a lie and he was consumed and controlled by secrets and lies. Whenever God tried to call him to repentance or work in his life, he absolutely refused. He was angry with God and living totally out of submission to God's will. If he ever was really saved, I believe at this point he was backslidden. Combine that with the plethora of evil, demonic influences that were in his life, and he was wide open for demonic control.

And when they controlled, he was completely out of his mind.

Sometimes he'd just stare off into space for hours. Other times he'd erupt in anger and violence. With a demonic look in his eye, he'd say the most hateful, horrible things.

Another tactic he'd use to abuse our mom was to go after weak areas in her health. It was a tactic that had worked throughout their marriage—whenever they'd disagree he'd give her the silent treatment, punish her, sometimes even starve himself. Eventually, her irritable bowel syndrome (IBS) would kick in from the tension and she'd give him whatever he wanted just to get out of pain.

We didn't recognize it as abuse then, but when he used the same tactics to raise her blood pressure to dangerous levels or put her lungs in jeopardy by ignoring her severe environmental allergies, it became clear that this was a form of abuse. Eventually, we realized that Mom could not be left alone with him. In fact, as a general rule, we decided that none of us should ever be alone with him.

For many years, this was a major component of our lives. In fact, most of my dad's abusive behavior didn't stop until Mom died. For almost fifteen years we lived under the threat of his mood swings, temper tantrums, violence, anger, and attempts at making Mom sick.

Many people ask, "Why didn't you leave?"

Honestly, I would not recommend that any other women follow our example and stay. However, because of Mom's extreme environmental allergies, moving was not an option. Just going to the store or sitting in traffic was difficult.

Would she have left if she could have?

I don't know . . . probably not. She loved Dad and always believed that God could do something to change him. As the secrets and lies poured out we understood more and more of why he was acting the way he did, and we wanted to see him walk the road to healing. Unfortunately, he chose to fight it. In the end, because of her health, she couldn't leave and Jamie and I wouldn't leave her alone.

Instead, God gave us the grace, courage, and protection to live in this extremely difficult circumstance. Along the way, he used all of this to heal the deepest wounds in our hearts—

the secret abuse that we didn't know was going on our whole lives.

Although it seems strange to say, the truth is that the majority of the damage that was done to our heart, minds, and spirits didn't come from the physical abuse. Instead, we spent years in prayer and counseling working through and overcoming the much more damaging emotional and mental abuse that we experienced throughout our lives.

Don't kid yourself—emotional abuse is just as damaging, if not more damaging, than physical abuse because rather than attacking your body that can heal, emotional abuse attacks the very core of who you are. That's what Mom, Jamie, and I spent years working with the Holy Spirit to heal and overcome.

You see, it was an interesting thing. As long as everything looked perfect on the outside, we didn't understand how much emotional and mental abuse was going on behind closed doors.

Yet once "perfect" was blown away and we were forced to live in this nightmare situation, that's when the Holy Spirit was able to really shine his light and help us see that this wasn't a new thing. Abuse had played a prominent role for years and if we wanted to be truly healed, we had to acknowledge it, be delivered from it, and learn to live differently.

I guess you could say our journey to overcoming abuse started on New Year's Day 1998.

I don't remember what started it, but sometime around 8 or 9 o'clock at night my dad's anger got completely out of control. Jamie was home from college and he just couldn't stand how Dad was treating Mom and eventually they got into a physical fight.

Chapter 5 ～ Abuse

Eventually, my dad went to stay at a relative's house until he could calm down.

The next day, we began searching for a Christian treatment center to help him deal with his issues. However, because he wasn't struggling with drugs or alcohol, he could only get help on an out-patient basis.

The nightmare continued when Dad went to a new counselor who believed the lies, and essentially told him it was time to "drop the hammer" on his family. I still remember the day that Dad came home from a counseling session and told my mom and I that this was the way things were going to be and if we didn't like it we could move out of HIS house.

We did leave, for a scheduled doctor's appointment, and to get away for awhile. We didn't even know if we were welcome to go back home, but having nowhere else to go, we returned. When we got home, we found Dad sitting on the floor in my brother's room, staring at the wall like a zombie. It was impossible to get him to react in any form. It was terrifying.

I don't remember how that evening ever resolved itself. The next thing I remember is that Mom and I were asked to come into the counselor's office, where every problem in our family was blamed on us. It was horrifying being told that the erratic behavior, the violence we'd been experiencing, and the uncontrollable anger were our fault. We left that office completely devastated and wondering if God, like the counselor, was against us, blamed us, and had abandoned us.

That night when Dad came home from work, he was brokenhearted at what the counselor had done to us. He knew as well as we did that the problems were not our fault; he just had no idea what to do to solve them. He made us dinner and decided that he was done with yet another counselor. That night, he was the man I knew growing up, not the out-of-control, demonically controlled man he'd become.

The next day, he went to work and Mom, totally disillusioned, decided to make one last ditch attempt at finding help. She called Rev. Richard Herritt, a local pastor who had experience in spiritual warfare and deliverance ministry. Seeing the demonic element in my dad's abuse, this pastor was able to help us by helping Dad.

We soon realized whenever my dad was having one of his episodes, rather than trying to rationalize with him or responding in our own fear and anger, he needed the outside help of a counselor who specialized in deliverance. It was the only thing that got him back under control.

Meanwhile, the Holy Spirit continued to work in us, setting us free.

Despite my dad's best efforts to keep them hidden, truth was coming to the surface. Each member of our family—Mom, Jamie, and I—began seeing how Dad's choices influenced us. Through the light of the Holy Spirit, we started to see how things that we thought were normal were actually very abnormal.

In time, we all came to learn that behind closed doors, he was not the man he claimed to be. Instead, he was a man who was filled with hate and rage. He also had a lot of issues with women.

At some point in his life he decided that he was not going to hurt again. Instead, he was going to control everyone and everything in his life through guilt, manipulation, and emotional, physical, verbal, and mental abuse.

Throughout our lives, Mom took the worst of the abuse, but she didn't recognize it as abuse because it wasn't the drunken beatings with which she associated abuse. Dad's tac-

Chapter 5 — Abuse

tics were very different and deceptive; still, she was abused in every way. Whenever possible, he would demean her, blame her, and make her feel bad about herself so that she would remain under his control.

She had very little freedom in their marriage. He almost hovered over her.

He didn't like her to have women friends. He was a loner and he wanted to keep her all to himself. He also didn't want her to see "normal" and begin questioning our lives. We eventually learned that isolation is common in abuse situations.

He kept strict tabs on where she was and what she was doing.

She didn't have a say in managing money, but lived in money darkness. He gave her money, but he also gave her a list of chores to "earn the money."

He made rules that she had to follow, but they didn't apply to him.

She didn't have a car, so that limited her freedom. She very seldom shopped by herself, including grocery stores, department stores, and furniture stores. In his eyes, she couldn't do anything good enough. He always corrected her and showed her how to do it his way. In the end, she lived in a lot of stress all of the time.

The sad thing is that for most of our lives, she suffered alone and in silence, trying to provide my brother and I with a safe, happy, healthy environment in which to grow up. For the most part, she was successful.

It wasn't until Jamie and I were in our twenties and the Holy Spirit pointed his spotlight on our lives that we learned how much she had really suffered and been abused over the

Finding Healing

years. Although we aren't going to discuss everything, it's safe to say that she suffered abuse in every area of her life.

Of course, it turns out that when the secrets started coming out, it wasn't just Mom who had been abused. My brother had his own stories of secret physical abuse, accompanied with, *"Don't tell your mom, she'll get angry. You know she doesn't love you and if we get divorced you'll have to live with me. What are you going to do then?"*

This was just the tip of the iceberg of the mental and emotional abuse Jamie experienced as Dad secretly turned him against Mom. We learned later this is a form of parent alienation syndrome.

I took the least abuse because my dad didn't like me. Because of his childhood he had a general hatred toward women—especially women with a strong personality, desire to succeed, and goal-oriented mindset. That was me!

We spent very little time together. When we were together, he made it clear that nothing I did pleased him, I wasn't a good daughter, I wanted too much out of life, and I was the problem who needed to change. Unfortunately, my dad and I were together enough for him to influence my attitudes toward myself and relationships between men and women. By the time I went to college I was accustomed to accepting abuse and was only interested in men with controlling, abusive personalities.

Like others who had come before me, I had been conditioned to accept and expect abuse and had a very unhealthy image of how women were to be treated. So I understand why women take abuse—they think it's normal. It's all they know, and they think it's what they deserve.

Thankfully, although these are the facts of our story, this is not the end of our story.

As our family went to counseling to deal with these issues, we were also able to get to the heart of our issues with abuse, experience healing, break the cycle, and learn to live free from abuse. We learned that there is power in the name of Jesus to break the chains that bind—even of abuse. Even though I'd never be so naïve as to say it's an easy process or that there's a 1–2–3 formula, I would like to offer some of the steps that helped us overcome and live abuse-free.

Along the Way, Here's What We Learned

Face the truth.

Like I said, for many years, we did not face the truth about our lives. We thought everything was "perfect."

While preparing to write this chapter, I was reading through some of the old articles my mom wrote in the early days of our ministry. Here's what she said about facing truth:

> It has taken years for me to confess that I am an abused woman. I don't think I've ever done that before. Ignore it, make excuses, yeah, but openly admit it—this is new. It's hard to say it and even harder to admit it. But I want to be free and be the woman God wants me to become. I can't allow abuse to stop that.
>
> Any woman reading this who is abused knows how difficult it is to admit this truth. But we must. We need those chains off of us so we can be free. It is God's will for us to be free. We must change our minds so we can become normal and our lives give glory to God.

Admitting to yourself that there is a problem is one of the biggest hurdles for abused women to overcome. Instead, we want to blame ourselves or think that if we acted differently there would be no problem. Sometimes women will even say these words to friends who try to tell them, *"This isn't normal or right, you have to change."* Yet until the individual who is being abused admits that there is a problem, there is very little that can be done to help them.

> Talking breaks the cycle of secrets and secrets are the ropes that hold abusive relationships together.

For instance, I still remember the day that I was driving home from church and the Holy Spirit kept bringing up memories of cruel, hurtful things Dad had said to me. (Just because I didn't take a lot of physical abuse, doesn't mean the verbal abuse I received didn't do its damage.)

Even all these years later, I can recall the mental struggle between, **"This can't be true—I grew up in a Christian home,"** and the reality of the memories that were pushing their way to the forefront in my mind. It wasn't until I finally agreed with the Holy Spirit that my relationship with my father was very abusive that I could start to seek help and healing.

Break the silence.

I know this is tricky.

You're always afraid that people won't believe you or that the person who is abusing you will get angry and punish you.

You don't want to be the one to "muddy the waters" because then you'll have to deal with the consequences. Trust me, I know.

Honestly, only you know the true danger of your situation. You know if you can talk to a family member, friend, or pastor, or if you need to go to the police or talk to someone with a background in domestic violence. But the important thing is that **you need to talk to someone.** Don't keep this secret all to yourself. If you are living in an abusive, dangerous situation, go and talk to someone with experience who can get you some help.

If you are out of imminent danger and simply trying to work through the cycle of accepting abuse, then you, too, need to talk to someone and get some help.

Talking breaks the cycle of secrets; secrets are the ropes that hold abusive relationships together.

You cannot break free from abuse if you allow yourself to stay alienated and alone. Instead, find trusted individuals who can help you overcome not just the abuse but the twisted thinking that wants to accept abuse. Pray for a safe person with whom to talk. God can bring that person to you or impress upon you whom you can trust.

Get some help.

Although breaking the silence about abuse is important, it is really only the beginning of the journey. The next step is to seek the help of a Christian counselor who is trained in helping women overcome the issues in their hearts and minds that caused them to accept abuse.

You see, in an abuse situation, although it is not the victim's fault, if the victim wants to stop being victimized, she needs to get some help to break the cycle of abuse and ensure that she does not become the victim again. For our family, breaking this cycle included dealing honestly with the issues of our past (including my parents' past), seeking counseling, and even going through spiritual deliverance sessions with a trained minister.

It didn't happen overnight. We gained ground little by little as we persevered through the memories, doing a lot of talking, choosing to apply forgiveness, and learning new ways of thinking and living. Yet, with each counseling session we gained more ground and experienced more freedom leading to healthier lives.

Deal with the conditioning.

Did you know that your soul can crave abuse like an alcoholic craves alcohol?

If you were abused as a child or raised in an abusive household, then abuse is normal to your soul. You will feel safe and loved in abusive situations and you are conditioned to accept abuse. This training is something that you will need to be delivered from and work on overcoming.

Did you know that there is a generational aspect to abuse?

For many, once you've experienced abuse, there's a natural tendency to either abuse or accept abuse. Basically, hurting people hurt people. That's why it's so important that each of us chooses to break the cycle and addiction to abuse in our own lives.

The truth is that if great-grandma, grandma, and Mom accepted abuse or were abusers, then there is a high probability that you will be prone to follow in their footsteps. In fact, most of the time, people who abuse have experienced abuse themselves. It could be from a parent, a teacher, a neighbor, a friend—really anyone.

As the Holy Spirit was healing my heart, I began to see that Dad's attitudes toward women and how he treated Mom created a longing for abuse inside of me. I was drawn to abuse. I felt most comfortable around men who were like my dad and who treated women badly. Because of Dad's abuse over the years, I thought this was what I deserved, and this was how I defined love.

Part of my journey to overcoming abuse meant recognizing that abuse was a generational, learned behavior in our family. Left unaddressed, it would continue to go on and on.

The truth is that too many women continually end up in abusive relationships because they don't take the time to deal with the issues in their own hearts that draw them toward abusive men. Yet, what I found is that it wasn't until I realized that I had a problem—I was conditioned to accept abuse—and started working on my own heart that I was able to begin to overcome.

How do you start?

Soak your mind in God's Word and your heart in prayer.

Anyone who has lived through abuse knows that there's more to it than just the physical pain. That's only a small part. The real beatings come to your mind, soul, and spirit. That's why you're willing to accept the physical pain—you're already beaten down in every other area.

That's why it's so important that your road to recovery includes soaking your mind in God's Word on a daily basis and allowing the truth and light in the Word to heal your heart and reveal your true value as God's daughter. As you read the Bible, it will renew your mind, shining God's light into the twisted thinking and speaking truth into the dark areas of your soul.

I remember Mom saying that one of the things that helped her on her journey to freedom from abuse was memorizing Scripture. A few of the verses that helped her were:

> Isaiah 46:3–4: **"Listen to me, you descendants of Jacob, all the remnant of the people of Israel, you whom I have upheld since your birth, and have carried since you were born. Even to your old age and gray hairs I am he, I am he who will sustain you. I have made you and I will carry you; I will sustain you and I will rescue you."**

> Isaiah 49:15–16: **"Can a mother forget the baby at her breast and have no compassion on the child she has borne? Though she may forget, I will not forget you! See, I have engraved you on the palms of my hands; your walls are ever before me."**

> Isaiah 54:4–6: **"Do not be afraid; you will not be put to shame. Do not fear disgrace; you will not be humiliated. You will forget the shame of your youth and remember no more the reproach of your widowhood. For your Maker is your husband—the Lord Almighty is his name—the Holy One of Israel is your Redeemer; he is called the God of all the earth. The Lord will call you back as if you were a wife deserted and distressed in spirit—a wife who married young, only to be rejected," says your God."**

> Isaiah 61:1–4: **"The Spirit of the Sovereign Lord is on me, because the Lord has anointed me to

preach good news to the poor. He has sent me to bind up the brokenhearted, to proclaim freedom for the captives and release from darkness for the prisoners, to proclaim the year of the Lord's favor and the day of vengeance of our God, to comfort all who mourn, and provide for those who grieve in Zion—to bestow on them a crown of beauty instead of ashes, the oil of joy instead of mourning, and a garment of praise instead of a spirit of despair. They will be called oaks of righteousness, a planting of the Lord for the display of his splendor. They will rebuild the ancient ruins and restore the places long devastated; they will renew the ruined cities that have been devastated for generations."

You see, it's only as we begin to see ourselves through the eyes of our heavenly Father and find our identity in him that we begin to understand we do not deserve to be abused. Even though your abuser may have told you you're worthless, no good, and deserve everything you get, this is a lie.

The only way to get these lies out of your brain is to flood your mind with the truth of God's Word.

Read it. Meditate on it. Listen to it as you're falling asleep at night.

Focus on verses that tell you how God feels about you and how much he loves you so that you can overcome the lies of your abuser.

I know it sounds like an easy answer—almost a cliché—but it really is the best way to overcome abuse.

Forgive your abuser.

I know it sounds absolutely impossible—almost ludicrous—but a lesson that we've learned is that one of the keys to overcoming abuse is choosing to forgive every person that ever abused you in the past.

This doesn't mean that you are saying what they did to you was right. Instead, when you forgive those who abused you, you're releasing yourself from all the anger, hate, and feelings of revenge that you are carrying toward them.

As long as you hold on to these feelings, they are still controlling you and hurting you. However, when you set them free and put them in God's hands, you're really cutting the cords they have on you so that you can walk in freedom.

I know we're just touching the tip of the iceberg when it comes to forgiveness here. We discuss this much more in depth in the second half of the book in chapter 14, including how it feels to forgive, the mental barriers we have to overcome, and practical ways to forgive those who have deeply hurt you. We know forgiveness isn't easy—still it's necessary if you want to be free.

Learn to walk in freedom.

One of the biggest challenges for those who are accustomed to abuse is learning to walk in freedom. I know it was one of the biggest obstacles for my mom, my brother, and me. It's hard because over the years your brain forms a natural groove toward keeping the peace, being controlled, keeping your abuser happy, and accepting the blame when your abuser isn't happy. It's like learning to live in a cage.

Then someone opens the door and says, "You're free."

It's pretty normal for your natural response to be, "Now what?" You might even be afraid to take those first few steps out of the cage and into the big, wide world around you.

So how do you do it?

One step at a time.

Each day you put one step in front of the other and take another step toward freedom, knowing that even the smallest baby steps are getting you closer to your goal.

Build a support system.

Another key to learning to walk in freedom is having a support system around you, encouraging you to take each step forward and speaking words of life into your spirit.

For example, I remember many years ago, Jamie and I were on a day trip away from our home when what was formerly Dad's demanded dinnertime rolled around. Growing up, it was expected that a hot meal would be on the table every night when he walked through the door or else. Well, as the clock pushed toward that hour and it became apparent that I was not going to get home in time to cook, I began to panic. I could feel myself getting physically sick because the training in my brain said, "You're a bad daughter."

Fortunately, Jamie was there to provide a support system that said, "'Des, this isn't normal. Your dad is a grown man and he can cook for himself while you're out of town." Then he reminded me of the words that our counselor was trying to teach us about walking in and enjoying God's freedom rather than accepting abuse. That day with the help of my support system, I was able to take a baby step toward walking in freedom.

Now, years later, I don't even feel a twinge of guilt when I tell my dad, "You're on your own tonight, I'm going out."

Healthy thinking has replaced abuse and I'm now living in freedom.

But it started one step at a time, choosing to step out of the cage and walk free from abuse.

Today, if you're reading this and you're suffering under the terror of abuse, I hope this chapter encourages you to take your own steps out of the cage and into freedom. Whether it be admitting to yourself that you need help, breaking your silence, seeking help, or making the choice to forgive and walk in freedom, I encourage you that today is the day to start.

Don't continue being the victim of another person's unresolved issues. Instead, take personal responsibility and decide that you are going to take your own first baby steps to freedom.

As someone who has taken the journey to freedom and overcome, I can tell you it is well worth every effort.

Chapter 6

Lies

After the Christmas that changed our lives, Dad started going to counseling. Over the next year, he saw about a dozen different counselors, not really finding many answers.

The pattern was always the same. He'd meet a counselor and they'd start making progress. Then all of a sudden Dad would find something wrong with that counselor and he'd have to find a new one. On and on this pattern continued until we found ourselves in the counselor's office at a prominent Assemblies of God church.

It was December of the next year when Dad's counselor asked to see Mom first, then us.

In his session with Mom he asked a question that she'd never considered before: *"What are you going to do if your husband doesn't change?"*

She didn't have an answer but was shocked by the possibility.

That's when the counselor revealed to us some of the problems he saw in Dad that we were completely oblivious to until that time.

The biggest revelation was that Dad was a pathological liar.

Although we lived to see that the counselor was indeed correct, in the moment it rocked our world.

How could this be possible?

What was Dad lying about?

What was happening to our perfect world?

As time passed and more and more secrets revealed themselves, we realized this was true.

Over time, we found out that he lied about his past, his family, his job, his income, our finances, and our lives.

We also learned that the things he told us about ourselves that were tying us into knots were lies. One by one each of those lies had to be revealed, sorted through, forgiven, and we had to learn how to walk in truth.

As the counselor explained, it wasn't that Dad meant to be a deceitful person or even knew he was lying. In response to trauma that he wouldn't face or deal with, he created an imaginary world where lying and making things look better than they were became his default setting. One of the biggest obstacles that we had to face was that he sincerely believed his lies and had suppressed the truth so deeply.

This became our new truth as lie upon lie and secret upon secret began to be revealed.

But this is just a portion of our story regarding lying. I wish it was the only part, but being completely open and honest, I have to admit that finding out about our dad's lies revealed an issue in our own hearts.

What my brother and I soon had to admit was that by living with a liar for all of those years, we had picked up this trait and were starting to allow lying to be a part of our lives.

Chapter 6 — Lies

By the time we were in our late teens and early twenties, it was a big sin that both Jamie and I needed to overcome.

The two biggest areas where we struggled with lying were:

1. Lying to stay out of trouble or avoid causing trouble
2. Lying to make ourselves or our lives look better than they actually were.

Looking back, it's easy to see that the first area was the result of the extreme pressure we lived under for things to always be perfect. (Maybe it was the same in Dad's life.) When the drama, blame, and punishment were so great for every little infraction that rocked the boat, it was just easier to lie than face the music.

I remember talking to my mom about this once. I was apologizing for lying about going out with my friends to the mall in college when I was told not to go, and her saying, *"Lying is wrong and you shouldn't have done it, but that was a stupid rule and there was way too much manipulation and control over our lives."*

So while I'm not excusing it (because it was wrong), this was the cause.

The other type of lying fell right into my dad's footsteps. The truth is that we and our lives were boring. To impress people and fit in, we exaggerated stories, made ourselves look more exciting, and created a world that was bigger than reality. It was when we realized that we had fallen into that trap and were following in my dad's destructive footsteps that we stopped dead in our tracks and decided lying had to go.

Immediately, if not sooner.

The consequences we were living with every day were so dramatic and so awful that we both decided this was a sin and generational iniquity that was going to die. We were going to do whatever it look to kill it.

Along the Way, Here's What We Learned

It doesn't matter why you lie or how you lie, any form of lying and deceit is a sin.

The Bible is very clear on God's feelings about lying and deceit. It is one of his Ten Commandments. He hates it!

Proverbs 12:22 (ESV) says, **"Lying lips are an abomination to the Lord."**

That's a pretty strong statement about what God thinks of deceit and lying!

The Bible says that liars cannot get into heaven (Psalms 101:7).

Revelation 21:8–9 lists liars with the "big sinners"—murderers, the sexually immoral, witches, and idol worshippers. I'm pretty sure that means God has an issue with us lying and being deceitful.

As we learned in our own lives, nothing can be more devastating to our walk with God than lies and deceit.

When I think of an example of a man who almost lost it all because of deceit, Jacob springs to my mind. If anyone's life is an exposé on the consequences lying, it would be him.

As we read through his life (Genesis 25–37), we see that lying was his default setting whenever he was in trouble. It was also the source of most of his pain and heartache.

We see it start when he lied to his father, pretending to be his brother, to receive the promised blessing and birthright.

Although he got what he wanted, he also lost his home when he had to flee to Laban and work as a servant rather than a son. He had to leave his beloved mom and he never saw her again. She died before he returned. Deceit cost Jacob his closest relationship. He left home alone and broke.

Jacob went to live with his Uncle Laban. While living there, he fell in love with Rachel, Laban's daughter. He traded seven years of his life in hard labor to Laban for the privilege of marrying her. At the end of these years, Jacob's deceitful past came back full circle. He found himself on the receiving end of a con job orchestrated by Laban when on the wedding night, Laban switched daughters on Jacob.

The con man had been conned!

However, Jacob was not to be outdone. He returned to an old pattern of deceit to get what he wanted. He devised a scheme to get rich. He used an old shepherd's trick to con Laban and make himself richer.

Laban's sons were outraged at the way Jacob duped their father. When Jacob heard of their anger, he packed up his family and ran away in the middle of the night. Once again Jacob's deceit cost him a place to call home.

Jacob spent his entire life practicing deceit. He never trusted God to take care of him. He didn't wait for God to vindicate him or work things out. However, it never worked out.

As a matter of fact, it got worse. His deceitful ways were handed down to his sons.

Jacob's son's used deceit to get revenge on an entire city (Genesis 38). Again Jacob was forced to run away. This time the trip cost him his beloved wife Rachel, who was pregnant. She died in labor, exhausted from the hasty departure. Deceit took Jacob's mother, his wife, and any home he ever had.

It still didn't end.

After the death of Rachel, Jacob turned all of his love and attention to Rachel's son Joseph. He spoiled Joseph and made him the favorite son, causing his other sons to hate Joseph. They despised the favoritism and love he received from their father. Their hatred drove them to sell Joseph into slavery.

How did they tell Jacob the news about Joseph? They used their father's favorite method. They lied to their father about what they had done to Joseph. They told Jacob that an animal had killed him. They even dipped Joseph's coat in blood as part of their lie.

Jacob, not knowing the truth, felt he had lost it all. Jacob's sons used lies and deceit, just like Jacob had done to Esau so many years ago. Deceit cost Jacob his mother, his wife, and now his son.

Deceit never brings about a happy ending. Jacob learned this lesson the hard way. Looking at his life and legacy we see that lying is a big deal and the consequences can be devastating.

Of course, Jamie and I didn't need to learn from Jacob's life. We were seeing up close and personal the devastation that comes from secrets and lies. That was all we needed to ask: **How can we overcome the sin of lying and learn to walk in truth?**

Here are practical ways that we overcame this deadly sin.

First, we had to confess that lying was a sin in our lives.

This wasn't exactly easy to admit to ourselves or anyone else. After all, Jamie was in Bible college at this time, and I'd just graduated Bible college and was seeking God's will for future ministry.

Even more, we really loved Jesus. We were committed Christians who loved God and wanted to devote our entire lives to him. Yet, somehow this deadly sin had fallen between the cracks in our lives.

I guess we didn't see it as that big of a deal.

So we exaggerated a little? So we told a little white lie to get out of trouble? Everybody does it right? What's the harm?

Well, the harm was that lies were a huge contributing factor in my dad's downfall and our family's painful history. When the Holy Spirit brought this to light and pointed out that if we didn't change, we, like Jacob and his sons, were going to keep the destructive pattern going, we saw the gravity of the situation.

Confession must be a priority.

First, we started by confessing to God.

Individually, we made lists of all the times we could remember lying, all the way back to when we were kids. After the lists were made each of us in our own time of prayer confessed each of these sins to God and asked him to forgive us. Although this might seem a little overboard to some, to us, it was necessary because we wanted every single fragment of lying out of our lives.

Next, we started confessing to each other.

We talked among our family about our struggle with lying. We admitted times we lied to each other, and asked forgiveness.

The biggest effect that confession had on our lives was that it created an atmosphere of accountability. Knowing that we struggled with this issue, we were holding each other accountable to always be truthful.

Speak no lies.

Another thing we each did to get every trace of this sin out of our lives was committing to speaking only what was true. If we spoke anything that was not 100 percent accurate, we would have to go back and correct it. When we say anything, I mean ANYTHING!

We were so zealous that I would correct the most minute details. We would correct statements, even if it was as simple as saying something "took me five minutes" and it actually took me six. Again, it might seem overboard, but we were committed to overcoming.

Looking back, one of the biggest practical methods that helped us overcome lying was the process of making restitution. For instance, I remember one time in college I lied to avoid paying a fine for skipping chapel. When we were dealing with overcoming lying, I felt so convicted that I wrote the Student Life office a letter of apology and paid the fine.

It was humiliating! But God asked me to do it, so I did it.

Let me tell you, this kind of action kills sin inside of you pretty quickly! With a lot of hard work, repentance, and humility, we were

> *One of the practical methods that helped us overcome lying was the process of making restitution.*

able to conquer and defeat this monstrous enemy of deceit that had been given a foothold in our lives.

It's time to come clean.

Today, if you are caught in the trap of lies, we urge you to follow our example and do whatever it takes to set yourself free.

You might be thinking, "But you don't understand. I've told some really big lies. When I tell the truth the consequences are going to be pretty dramatic."

Actually, we do understand. Remember, we lived though the dramatic consequences of finding out about all of our dad's lies. Yet, I promise you this: **As hard as it is to tell the truth and face the music, it will be even harder if the truth finds out and you're caught in lies you haven't confessed.**

If you are lying, you need to come clean and face the truth.

Perhaps you will need to find a counselor first who can help you tell the truth and help you know how to face the consequences. But the important thing is that you start walking in truth—complete truth today.

John 8:32 says, **"You will know the truth and the truth will set you free."**

Freedom is on the other side of lies. You overcome by becoming a person of truth.

Chapter 7

Shame

"So what happened? Didn't you learn anything at that college you went to that you came home without a job?"

We were standing in the middle of a store when the cashier, a mother to a high school friend, asked this question. It took three days before Mom insisted I leave the house again.

Then there was the day that a neighbor came to "comfort" my mom over the fact that I'd graduated college without a husband. *"We all just feel so sorry for her; I mean what is she going to do?"*

I was the ripe old age of twenty-two and could hear every word from inside the door.

For the first time in my life, I experienced real shame.

Up until this time most of the people I knew thought highly of me. It seemed like I was the girl on the move—going places, getting out of my small little town, and destined to live happily ever after.

Growing up, my visions were to come back home the conquering hero. Instead I returned home a failure.

As you've already read, it was not a warm reception.

People were more than thrilled to see the first chink in the armor of the perfect family.

Even though this was all part of God's perfect plan for me to come home so that I could start dealing with the issues in my heart, seeing the truth about our family, and becoming who God wanted me to be, from the outside it didn't look that way.

I looked like a failure and I was drowning in shame.

Over the next decade, as God continued leading our family through the healing process, we all continued to struggle with this suffocating monster.

There was the shame of being a failure.

Jamie felt shame that he wasn't a "real man" because his disability didn't allow him to play sports and be an outdoorsman. I struggled with the shame of not fulfilling my natural role as a woman as a wife and mother.

Then there was the shame of how abnormal our lives appeared to the outside world.

Shame that we were no longer perfect.

There was shame attached to the lies and secrets. I mean, how could we have been so deceived about our own lives?

All of us experienced the shame that comes hand in hand with abuse as you're always told, "It's your fault. This wouldn't be happening if you were different. You deserve to be treated this way."

Seriously, this was a big issue—shame was stealing our lives.

Thankfully, God stepped in and said, "Enough is enough."

Chapter 7 ⋒ Shame

Along the Way, Here's What We Learned

Shame comes in all shapes and sizes.

I recently heard *shame* defined as *"a sense deep inside that there is something fundamentally wrong with you."*

The Free Dictionary defines it as a painful emotion caused by a sense of guilt, embarrassment, unworthiness, or disgrace.

It can be a mix of regret, self-hate, and dishonor.

Dr. Kristalyn Salters-Pedneault defines shame as, *"An emotion in which the self is perceived as defective, unacceptable, or fundamentally damaged. Shame is often confused with guilt, which is related but distinct emotion in which a specific behavior is viewed as unacceptable or wrong, rather than the entire self. People who experience traumatic events are prone to shame, particularly if they blame themselves for the event. Shame can be a particularly problematic emotion because it is associated with a desire to hide, disappear, or even die."*[1]

Here's the thing I've learned about shame: Often we associate these things with "big sins." We tend to think that only people who've lived a super-sinful life understand what shame feels like.

We define shame as feeling regret for things we've done.

But what I've learned about shame is that it comes in all shapes and sizes and clings to people of all backgrounds and cultures. The truth is that the church member who's spent every week of his or her life inside of the church can be struggling with just as much shame and insecurity as a person with a colorful past.

Personally, I grew up in the church. I became a Christian when I was five years old and answered the call to ministry when I was eight years old. My mom raised my brother and me to know right from wrong and because of her strict rules I never really got into any trouble.

Yet, I can tell you that my own struggle with shame, feelings of inadequacy, lack of value and self-worth was real.

Some feel shame because of their weight or their appearance.

Others experience shame because of their lack of education or job experience.

Many experience shame because of their past or their family background.

The problem with shame is that it doesn't focus on any one demographic, but rather, it tries to attack at every economic, social, and age level pointing out either insufficiencies, insecurities, or the mistakes made in the past. Its goal is to cause you to be so overcome by the things you *aren't* or the things you've *done* that you become a prisoner.

Shame wants to control you.

It wants to make you hide away and never become the strong, godly, competent person that God created you to be.

That's really why the enemy of our souls uses this weapon on so many Christians. He's afraid of what they could become if they allowed Jesus to control their life rather than shame. He's afraid of the life they'd live, the people they'd influence, and the difference they could make among their family, their friends, their community, and ultimately for the kingdom of God.

The best way he knows to stop us is to attack us with shame. If he can make us feel unworthy, unloved, unwanted, and unnecessary there's always the chance that we'll agree with him and say, "You know what, that's right, I can't do what God wants me to do. I can't live the way God wants me to live and be who God's called me to be. Why am I even trying?"

It's one of the enemy's top strategies. However, thanks to Jesus, we can recognize this strategy and overcome it, throwing off the chains of shame once and for all and walking in the freedom of Jesus Christ.

How do we overcome shame?

Recognize shame for what it is: An attack of the enemy who wants to destroy us.

The first step in winning any battle is recognizing that you are at war.

When you are constantly being barraged with bombshells from an enemy, you are under attack. When you decide to fight back—you are at war.

For too long, Christians have allowed the enemy to constantly attack them with the lies of shame telling them they aren't good enough, they can never accomplish anything, they aren't worthy of God's love, and they have no potential. Because they are unwilling to fight the battle spiritually, lives are being destroyed and devastated by the enemy's terrorism.

However, this does not have to continue.

As God's children we can recognize that we are in a spiritual battle and choose to use the spiritual weapons that God has given us to fight against the lies of the enemy.

The first step toward this end is standing up and saying, "I recognize that this is a spiritual attack. The enemy wants to destroy me, but I'm not going to let him. Instead I'm going to use the sword of the Word of God to fight these lies and gain the victory."

Use the Bible to recognize your true identity as God's child.

Shame tells you all of the things that you are not. However, the truth of the Bible wants to tell you who you are: First and foremost, you are God's chosen child, holy and beloved.

I John 3:1 says, **"See what great love the Father has lavished on us, that we should be called children of God! And that is what we are!"**

Ephesians 1:3–5 & 11 says, **"Praise be to the God and Father of our Lord Jesus Christ, who has blessed us in the heavenly realms with every spiritual blessing in Christ. For he chose us in him before the creation of the world to be holy and blameless in his sight. In love, he predestined us for adoption to sonship through Jesus Christ, in accordance with his pleasure and will ... In him we were also chosen, having been predestined according to the plan of him who works out everything in conformity with the purpose of his will."**

Because God chose us and adopted us, we are literally now sons and daughters of the King of the universe. Even before you knew him, God chose you. He reached out to you.

He made a way through his Son Jesus Christ for you to be adopted and become his child.

God didn't choose you because of the things that you could or couldn't do.

He was never interested in the lists of what you are or what you're not. He didn't choose you because of your abilities, your appearance, your education, your financial status, or your relationship status.

1 Corinthians 1: 26–28 says, **"Brothers and sisters, think of what you were when you were called. Not many of you were wise by human standards; not many were influential; not many were of noble birth. But God chose the foolish things of the world to shame the wise; God chose the weak things of the world to shame the strong. God chose the lowly things of this world and the despised things—and the things that are not—to nullify the things that are."**

One of the best ways to fight an attack of shame is to come back with: "God still chose me to be his, and he still has a plan to fulfill in my life."

So what is the antidote to the lies of the enemy when shame wants to list all the things that you are lacking?

Well, it's to agree, with a twist.

The twist is that God doesn't care.

Even before you knew him, God chose you, and made a way through his Son Jesus Christ for you to be adopted and become his. And even knowing all of your faults and flaws, shortcomings and weaknesses, he still chose you and said, **"I know what they are not. But if they will surrender themselves to me and let me mold them into the image of my Son, Jesus Christ, and if they will obey me and follow the path I've laid out for their life—I am going to do amazing things with their life. Things that NOBODY could imagine. I'm not only going to revolutionize their life but I'm going to use them to start a revolution in my kingdom."**

In ourselves we really are nothing, but Jesus specializes in taking nothing and using it to bring glory to himself.

That's why one of the best ways to fight an attack of shame is to come back with: *"I may not be all of the things you are listing, but God doesn't care. He still chose me to be his child, and he still has a plan to fulfill in my life."*

Get to the root of the problem.

Whenever enemies declares war, they always start by finding areas that are the most vulnerable to attack—the weaknesses. One thing I've learned in my own life is that in my battle with shame, Satan always attacks in my weakest areas—where I'm most vulnerable.

That's why one of the keys to winning the battle against shame in our lives is getting to the root of the problem, dealing with it, and shoring up the weak areas.

For instance, in my own effort to overcome shame, I've had to face some issues in my past that created vulnerable areas in my soul and mind. On my journey, I've had to face the pain of rejection and abuse from my dad, and how his issues with women had a negative effect on my life.

Chapter 7 ~ Shame

For instance, one of the biggest areas where I struggled with shame was that I was ashamed of being single. On my journey to healing I discovered that one of the reasons that being single was such a vulnerable area for me is because my dad tied my type-A personality (which he didn't like) to whether or not any man would ever want me. I have clear memories of him telling me, "If you don't change, no man is ever going to want you."

Even though it was God's plan for my life to be single at this time, shame used my dad's words and the emotional pain that his words caused to create feelings of guilt, embarrassment, unworthiness, or disgrace.

The only way I could overcome my issues with shame was to face my past, forgive my dad, and realize that his words were skewed by his own issues from his past. Then, I had to accept the truth that God is in control of my life, that he created me just the way I am, and that he has a unique plan and purpose for my life.

Now I know that as long as I am living in God's plan and purpose, being single is no longer a source of shame. In fact, after years of God healing the pain of my past and helping me find my identity and purpose in him, I was able to do the previously unthinkable and not only find peace in my singleness, but also minister to single women. Still, I know that this never would have been possible if I hadn't faced the source of my shame and applied biblical principles to the root of my problem.

That's why I encourage you—if you're struggling with shame, allow the Holy Spirit to heal the root of the problem in your life.

If you need to go to a counselor to deal with your issues, then do it.

Finding Healing

Don't allow shame to control you. Instead, take control of it by going to the root and tearing it out, saying, "You're not going to control my life any longer. I will be free!"

Accept God's forgiveness and new life.

Another big weapon that the enemy uses to attack God's people with shame is reminding them of the sins of their past. Instead of reminding you of what you are not, he reminds you of what you were with lies like:

"There's no way you can serve God with your history."

"How do you ever expect to be used by God after what you've done or after what you've lived through?"

"You're never going to overcome this area of your life. It's going to haunt you and plague you for the rest of your life—you'll never be free. You might as well just give up now."

Again, the goal is to get you to stop moving ahead obediently with God's plan for your life and instead wallow in the chains of your past.

Once again—the key to overcoming is recognizing that this is a lie and choosing to fight shame with the truth of God's Word.

2 Corinthians 5:17 says, **"Therefore, if anyone is in Christ, the new creation has come: The old has gone, the new is here!"**

Isaiah 43:18–19 says, **"Forget the former things; do not dwell on the past. See, I am doing a new thing! Now it springs up; do you not perceive it? I am making a way in the wilderness and streams in the wasteland."**

Look at this truth from Romans 8:31–35:

Chapter 7 — Shame

> What, then, shall we say in response to these things? If God is for us, who can be against us? He who did not spare his own Son, but gave him up for us all—how will he not also, along with him, graciously give us all things? Who will bring any charge against those whom God has chosen? It is God who justifies. Who then is the one who condemns? No one. Christ Jesus who died—more than that, who was raised to life—is at the right hand of God and is also interceding for us.

No matter what happened in your past, you are not living there anymore. If you have repented and God has forgiven you, you're wholeheartedly following Jesus and allowing him to shape you into his image, then in God's eyes, the past is forgotten. When he looks at you now, he sees the blood of Jesus paid at Calvary. That's what it means to be *justified*—in God's eyes, it is just as if you have never sinned.

Because of this fact, Satan has no right to use the weapon of shame against you. You are a new creation, living a new life. That may have been who you were, but it is not who you are now. If you want to overcome shame, you need to accept Christ's forgiveness, forgive yourself for the past, and claim your new identity as God's child, living your life for his glory.

If you really want to defeat shame once and for all, share your testimony.

John 4 tells the story of the woman at the well. When we first meet her, she is absolutely covered with shame. Her shame had driven her into isolation—so much so that we meet her on her way to the well during the hottest, hardest time of day. It was the worst time of day to fetch water, but the only way that she could be sure she'd avoid people and hide in shame.

Then she had an encounter with Jesus. This encounter changed her life. He offered her something that she desperately needed—a way to change her life—to be free from her shame and start all over again. Although she initially wanted the living water that he offered, in the end, she accepted the new life that he gave when he told her that he was the Messiah.

That's when we see the most amazing thing happen. The conversation ends when the disciples return with the food. However, the story is not ending but taking a dramatic turn. Because somewhere during this woman's encounter with Jesus, she experienced a revolution.

Now instead of hiding in shame, she's actually going back into the town seeking people out.

Rather than avoiding people because of her past, she's telling everyone who will listen, "I just met a man who told me everything I've ever done—he's the Messiah."

Because of the encounter that she had with Jesus Christ, her life was revolutionized. What was formerly her shame was now her testimony as she fulfilled the plan that God had for her life—becoming the catalyst for a revival in her town.

> *If you want to overcome shame, you need to accept Christ's forgiveness, forgive yourself for the past, and claim your new identity as God's daughter.*

Over the years, fighting my own battle with shame, one thing I've learned is that whenever I choose to share the testimony of what Christ has done in my life, whenever I allow Christ to take the weak areas of my life and use them for his glory, shame has to run and hide.

Chapter 7 — Shame

Why?

Because all of shame's power is lost when you decide to come out of hiding, tell the truth, admit your area of weakness and say, *"Let the parts of my life that Satan wants to fill me with shame and use to devour me and my future, let them become a testimony of your faithfulness, of your mercy, of your power to intervene and bring life and freedom. God, if you can do anything with the ashes of my life, then feel free to make them beautiful."*

As I shared with you, all of the years of secrets and lies, abuse, and control caused our family to be filled with shame. Thankfully, the story doesn't end there. Instead, the story continued as God healed the broken areas of our lives and helped us find our true identity and purpose in him.

I hope this chapter inspires you to believe that shame can be overcome! Whatever its source, whatever role it's playing in your life, if you apply these steps to your own life, the Holy Spirit will be faithful and will deliver you from shame if you will cooperate with him and fight.

Freedom from shame is possible. I encourage you to start taking steps in that direction today.

> Whenever I choose to share the testimony of what Christ has done in my life, whenever I allow Christ to take the weak areas of my life and use them for his glory, shame has to run and hide.

Chapter 8

Finding Your Value

It was one of the hardest truths I had to face.

In his heart my dad was a deeply selfish man. Actually, he was a very damaged and broken man who at a very young age decided that he needed to take care of himself and make sure his needs were met. This carried into his adult life and marriage, meaning that he didn't get the normal sense of pride that comes with providing for a family. Instead, he saw it as a burden and resented it.

The result was that he came first. The rest of us made do.

When the Holy Spirit was working on my heart, healing my deepest wounds, one of the things he made me remember was the truth about the big box of clothes.

You see, when I was a little girl my mom always had an enormous box of clothes tucked away in the back of her closet. The box was filled with beautiful clothes that were passed down by a very generous aunt when my cousin outgrew them. Being quite the fashionista, my aunt only bought the best from the best stores, so they were really nice outfits.

Every spring and fall my mom would pull the box out of her closet and we'd have a "fashion show" as I tried on all

Finding Healing

the clothes to see which ones I'd grown into and could wear that season.

I loved this day! I, like the aunt who had given me the clothes, was a true "girly girl" who loved to dress up and get new things. My mom had such a way of making this day seem like a fun, special event that I completely enjoyed it and never really thought anything about the fact that all of my clothes were hand-me-downs.

That is until my cousin stopped growing and there were no longer any clothes coming in to fill the box.

That's when my mom sat me down to have a conversation.

I was about ten years old, maybe eleven, when my mom explained that we weren't going to be given anymore clothes. She talked to my dad and because we didn't have enough money to buy clothes, she would be making all of my clothes from now on. If I wanted things from a store, I had to earn the money and pay for them.

I remember feeling a little jolted by this conversation, but being a "rules girl" who always wanted to do the right thing, I told myself I'd just have to accept it. To a point I was trained to believe that this was right. Since a man worked, he needed lots of nice things. Because my mom didn't work, she contributed to the family by sewing all of her clothes, all of our curtains, bedspreads, pillows, and even sometimes new furniture cushions. It was her way of "earning her keep" and contributing.

This was the way God intended it to be. Now, if I wanted to be a good daughter and live in God's perfect will for a family, I had to submit to these new rules. So I did.

From that point forward Mom's workload increased as she now made all of my clothes, too. I started finding any little job I could get so that I would always have money to

Chapter 8 ~ Finding Your Value

buy the things I wanted. I also quickly found these amazing things called *sale racks* where you could get things really, really cheap. Saving money and scrounging for bargains became an obsession for me.

I thought this was normal—even right. Given the fact that my mom had amazing skills as a seamstress and she only copied the styles of the top designers, I always looked really good. The clothes were beautiful, stylish, and perfectly tailored to our specifications. This, too, fed my inner fashionista, so I didn't really see it as a problem. Oddly enough, we were actually proud of how beautiful our clothes were—that they were unique and not off the rack—and that we were saving so much money in the process.

Then the Holy Spirit started rocking our world.

When I was in college, all of the hours and years of sewing started causing my mom extreme physical pain. She'd developed spurs on her shoulders and spine that made each stitch painful. She no longer enjoyed sewing at all; it was now something she had to do or she and I would have no clothes.

Then one day on the way home from church the Holy Spirit spoke these words to her heart. He said, *"Kathy, I can provide for you and Adessa if you stop sewing. It's okay to give it up."*

These were life-changing words for my mom. Even though she didn't know how God would provide, she put the sewing machine aside and gave her body permission to heal.

We began the very difficult process of starting to shop for what we needed.

Now I know that many people will say, "Why is that difficult? Shopping is fun."

It isn't fun when you have been told your whole life that it is wrong and you don't deserve to have store-bought things

Finding Healing

or things that aren't clearance-rack-nobody-else-wants-them cheap. When your identity and value are actually tied to your ability to spend as little money and be as small of a burden as possible, learning to shop is an extremely painful process.

So painful, that there were several times when Mom tried to go back to sewing but just couldn't physically do it.

I avoided the pain by doing what I'd been told to do for years: earn your own money and pay for it yourself. Looking back, I can see that from the age of nine or ten, I always had a job and a little stash of my own money.

It started off that I'd clean for relatives or sell things. Then I added being an announcer at the local Little League games to my activities. Whether it was babysitting, cleaning, shoveling snow, or picking up odd jobs here or there, I knew that my value was tied to whether or not I had money. People with money deserved things—no money, you didn't deserve anything.

When it came time to go to college, the issue of money and value came up again.

You see, deep inside, my dad didn't want me to go to college. His thoughts that college was unnecessary and expensive combined with his issues with women and the end result was a battle. Of course, all of his arguments were disguised as a concerned father who didn't think I was "ready" for college, but the real heart of the matter was that he didn't want me to go and he didn't want to pay for it.

In the end, we compromised and I took a year off between high school and college to earn the money for my tuition. I worked as the faculty secretary's assistant at college and during the summer I had secretarial jobs to pay for my tuition. Although my dad did help a little bit, what I couldn't earn was eventually paid for by a relative who knew what I was going on with my dad and wanted to help. Meanwhile, Mom did her part by sewing me beautiful clothes and sewing everything I needed for my dorm room. She also cooked lots of meals that I took back to college and ate; she did everything she could to help me have a normal college experience. My great-grandmother gave me a television, and I had everything I needed.

Still, by this time I was living more and more with the conscious knowledge that as a woman I didn't deserve what a man did, and if I really wanted something I needed to find a way to pay for it myself.

When the Holy Spirit started healing the wounds inside of my heart and helping me find my identity in him, this was one of the first areas he went after.

It all began when I came home from college without a job.

This was a problem. No job . . . no money . . . no value.

Even though I really did want to surrender my will to God's will and commit to the healing process he wanted to take me through, my need for money and a sense of value was competing for my time. As no doors for ministry opened, I was always conjuring up some scheme to do short-term work and earn my own money. I even started substitute teaching for a while. Even though I was always applying for jobs at department stores or office jobs, God didn't allow any of these doors to open because he had a bigger agenda.

He wanted me to take an honest look at my life, see my dad for who he really was, and be healed and set free from all the pain and false images that came from my dad.

One of the first things I had to face was the truth about the big box of clothes.

I'm not sure that for me there was any memory that was more painful.

You see, all of my life I'd seen these clothes as a blessing. My mom really had an ability to make lemonade from lemons and she taught us to see everything as a gift and a blessing from God. Those clothes were a blessing because with or without my aunt's help, Dad wasn't going to sacrifice to provide for his family. These clothes provided for me and they kept my mom from having to keep up with the pressure of sewing clothes for a growing child.

Really, it wasn't the fact that I wore hand-me-downs that hurt—I honestly never saw it as a problem—it was the fact that my dad didn't want to provide for his daughter and his wife.

That reality was like a knife to the heart.

Soon I was able to see that it wasn't just clothes. The truth was that we did without a lot of things that were normal to other people. Anything that we had for the house, Mom had to sew or make herself. She couldn't buy anything.

Shoes were a big deal. I remember because Mom didn't work she could only have two pairs of shoes—one for church and one for leaving the house. They were always purchased for practically nothing and she had to make them last at least a year or it was a catastrophe. (I literally remember seeing my mom crying and panicking when a pair of shoes was accidentally ruined and she had to get new ones.)

Jamie and I were only given shoes as we needed and only at discounted prices. If I wanted the popular new shoes the other girls had, I had to pay for them with money I earned. Otherwise, they were too frivolous.

Even medicine or medical bills were a financial burden.

Chapter 8 — Finding Your Value

On and on the list could go of ways that my dad just did not want to meet our needs.

The more truth I faced, the more I had to deal with the question of, *"Why didn't my dad love me and want to provide for me?"*

That question broke my heart.

Looking back, I remember it being hard to even say it out loud in prayer at first. Literally forming the words was just too painful.

Eventually, I could talk to God about it and then to my mom and brother who were realizing the same things in their own lives at the same times. (I'm so glad that the Holy Spirit orchestrated our healings so that we could go through them together and not one person at a time.)

Mom remembered a time that her mother-in-law actually sat her down and explained that she needed to earn her keep as a wife.

We talked about the big box of clothes and my mom talked about how badly sewing hurt her body. As we had to move forward buying things rather than creating them, we'd talk about how hard it was, how we felt unworthy and even unloved, but how we knew we had to overcome and learn to be normal.

Ultimately, we talked about the need to find our value and identity in Christ and how we needed to learn to accept his love that couldn't be earned, couldn't be worked for, but could only be accepted even though it wasn't deserved.

Because ultimately, the issue of value had gone beyond clothes and seeped into every area of our lives.

Personally, I'd learned that love had to be earned—that I needed to prove to people that I was worth loving and having in their lives.

I'd developed a fierce independence where I knew I had to find a way to take care of myself—I even took pride in my independence.

Even in my relationship with God, I was trying to be "good enough" instead of resting in the fact that he loved me and wanted to provide for me whether I deserved his love or not.

This was a deep wound that piece by piece had to be prayed through, talked through, cried through, and ultimately step by step I had to overcome.

Along the Way, Here's What We Learned

Value cannot be earned.

It was a long hard struggle to get here, but ultimately, I had to learn that my value was not tied to my ability to earn money.

> *Value cannot be earned, rather it can only be found in finding your identity as God's daughter.*

Looking back, I believe that this is one of the reasons that God allowed me to go for so long without a job or any money of my own—he was starving this appetite out of me so that I had to find my value and identity in him.

I also had to learn that value could not be earned through work.

I remember days when I wasn't working and I had to rely on my mom (who was now administering the family budget after Dad's debt) to buy things for me. For the next few days, I'd be like superwoman cleaning the house, doing chores, making sure I was everyone's servant.

After a while, my mom caught on to what was happening and said, *"Stop! Do you realize that since you couldn't earn the money to pay for what you needed you're trying to pay me back in chores? This isn't right. You need to get alone with God and pray through this issue so you can overcome. You don't have to pay me back, but you do need to let God heal your heart so you don't feel like you always have to earn your keep."*

She recognized what was going on because she, too, was being set free from the same thing. In the end, we both had to realize that value could not be earned, rather it can only be found in finding your identity as God's daughter.

Freedom doesn't come without a fight.

When it comes to overcoming a stronghold or learned pattern that is this large in your mind, freedom isn't going to come without a fight. It isn't going to just magically happen.

Instead, you're going to have to take the attitude of Caleb in Joshua 14: Look your struggle in the eye like he looked at the giants in his land and say, "I know it won't be easy, but give me this mountain." We need to pursue our healing and freedom with passion!

What does this mean?

Well, for me, the first thing it meant was **facing the painful truth about our lives.**

I won't lie to you—it hurt. It was hard to have what were good memories dashed and torn apart. It was even harder facing the truth that my dad was so consumed with his own pain that he didn't want to provide for his family. Still, it wasn't until I allowed the Holy Spirit to show me this truth and remove it like a poison from inside of me that I could begin to heal.

Then, I had to **work through the steps of healing that are laid out in the later chapters of this book.**

I had to spend hours in prayer before God, dealing with the pain.

Then I had to engross myself in God's Word so that I could see my true value as his daughter.

We had to talk about the issue and then I had to forgive my dad.

All of these were really hard (as we talk about later in the book) and flooded me with emotions. Still, they were necessary for me to heal.

Finally, we had to learn to live differently.

Both my mom and I had to learn that we were worth having our needs met and that God wanted to provide.

And we had to learn to shop—for clothes, shoes, and household items and so many things. Part of our process was even learning to shop for furniture (also homemade until that point), appliances, and even buying cars. (Because remember, until we were set free neither Mom nor I had a car—we were girls and didn't need them.)

Please don't think we were by any means extravagant. Remember that at the same time we were paying off my dad's secret debt, learning to live by God's financial principles, and applying Dave Ramsey's *The Total Money Makeover*[1] principles to our lives. So we were and still are pretty frugal.

We weren't learning how to be spenders—we were learning how to live normally and it was a tough process. With each purchase we had to retrain our brains that it was okay to buy what you needed, God wants to provide for our needs, and if the money is there, it's okay to spend it.

We were also overcoming the lie that there was no money.

As truth came out we learned that my dad always had a good job and there always should have been enough money to live a decent middle-class life. The issues weren't "lack" but rather the selfishness in my dad's heart and his irresponsibility with money. When we learned how to handle money God's way, we learned there really was enough to provide for everyone's needs.

Part of fighting for our freedom was learning and realizing these truths. But even this required effort.

We had to relearn how to live and then we had to do what we were learning. It was a fight, but the freedom on the other side was so worth it!

Recognize your value.

Probably the biggest lesson I had to learn about value is that it comes from God.

It isn't dependent on what you do or don't do, what you are or aren't—it comes from God.

I wish I could give you an easy three-step method to discovering your God-given value, but the truth is that it only comes from spending time with him and in his Word.

It comes as the Holy Spirit shows you the things that are stealing your value.

This was my struggle. Yours may be different.

You may find your value in being pretty, skinny, smart, sexy, funny, easy to get along with, or successful at your job. You may have been taught that it comes from a relationship or someone else's approval. The truth is that we all find our value in different places.

Yet at the end of the day, none of these things actually make us feel valuable. They just keep us searching for significance and value. Ultimately, we become obsessed with the pursuit of these things because we need them to fill the void deep inside of our lives.

Yet what I have learned over the years is that the only thing that can end the obsessive race for self worth and fill the void that is screaming out in your life is a personal relationship with Jesus. A relationship that is more than just bedtime prayers and praying before dinner, but a relationship where you understand how deeply and passionately you are loved by God.

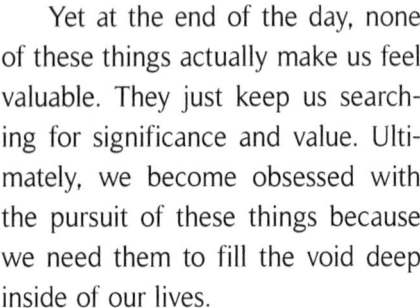

It's when you understand that you are valuable because God created you just the way you are—

- *you are valuable because he sent his son to die for your sins*
- *you are valuable because he has a purpose and plan for your life.*

—that's when you really start to find your identity.

Practically, how do you do that?

Spend time with Jesus and let him heal the wounds in your heart.

Chapter 8 — Finding Your Value

Spend time in the Bible studying who God is, how he feels about you, and who you are in him.

You see, the answer to the question, "What am I worth?" is found in the Bible. As we read it, meditate on it, and allow God's Word to answer this question, we will find that our true value and worth comes through being God's child.

As you trust your relationship with God enough to start allowing him to deal with the issues in your heart and mind that are stealing significance, bring them to the surface, heal them, and teach you how to overcome them, that's when you'll finally be able to conquer your own significance crisis and truly find your value in Jesus.

In the next chapter, we're going to go deeper into the topic of finding your identity as God's daughter.

However, we can't go too quickly into that topic without fully understanding the truth of this chapter: Your value is not tied to what you can do, what you can earn, what you can give someone else, how you look, how successful you are, or anything else that is "work" oriented.

> Your value is not tied to what you can do, what you can earn, what you can give someone else, how you look, how successful you are, or anything else that is "work" oriented.

The basic fact is **you are valuable.**

Not "because of" or "due to." As a human being created in the image of God and loved by God, you are valuable.

You are loved.

Finding Healing

    God wants to heal you from whatever has stolen your self-worth from you and restore your sense of value to you.

    Now the choice lies with you: Will you let him?

    Will you allow him to remind you of painful things?

    Will you let him heal your heart?

    Will you spend time with him and in his Word so that he can show you your true value?

Chapter 9

Finding Your Identity as a Child of God

We cannot wrap up our family's testimony and move on toward the practical steps to healing without discussing one last topic: the need to find your identity in Christ.

As you might imagine, finding our identity was a big part of our healing process. How could it not be?

Think about it: For years we believed our lives were a certain way. We thought we knew who we where and we derived our purpose and value from this identity.

Then "Boom!" Everything was different.

Even though we were on our way to finding truth, there were many years we felt like we were lost.

Everything we knew and believed was shaken.

Truths that we firmly believed were God's will were proven to be abusive distortions of God's perfect truth.

As we looked back on family memories and thought, "I simply had no idea what was happening, what those conversations really meant, or what that person was really thinking,"—we felt like our very core was being shaken.

I remember many times thinking or saying to my mom or brother, "This is really our lives?" It's all just so jolting.

Yet, even beyond the circumstances, there was another level of questioning.

After all the lies about who you were, how you should be, and even what God wants you to be are stripped away, you're left questioning:

If this is wrong, what is right?
Who am I really?
What is my real purpose?
What is God's true plan and design for my life?

What we learned on our road to healing is that when everything else is shaking, it's essential that you find your identity on the immovable unchangeable basis of God's truth.

> *All of us are called to find our identity, our place, and our purpose as God's children.*

The truth is that no matter what obstacle is standing in your past that needs to be healed or overcome, this lesson is a key element to finding your identity and significance and becoming the healthy person God wants you to be.

In fact, it may be one of the most important lessons of all, because the truth is that ALL of us are called to find our identity, our place, and our purpose as God's children. This is where we find who we are really called to be—our true identity—our true selves. It's when we truly grasp hold of the truth that this is our identity that we will finally be at peace with ourselves, at peace with our lives, and find our true passion and purpose in life no matter what our title.

John 1:12 says, **"Yet to all who did receive him, to those who believed in his name, he gave the right to become children of God."**

The Message says it this way:

But whoever did want him, who believed he was who he claimed and would do what he said, he made to be their true selves, their child-of-God selves.

Now, right up front, let me say that I understand that for many people when they hear the phrase or "child of God" there's an instant nervous reaction. Your back starts to tighten or you took a deep breath and braced yourself because it's really hard for you to hear the terms or "child" or "father" and relate to those terms in a good way.

Trust me, I get it.

When it came to the topic of dealing with God as a "Father"—well, even though I loved Jesus with all of my heart and wanted to serve him with everything in me—the topic of "father" was hard to relate to because the image of my earthly father was standing in the way.

From the bottom of my heart, I need to share with you that finding my true identity hidden within the title of being a child of God has been a life-changing experience that led to finding my true value, my passion, my place, and my purpose in life. It completely changed me, my outlook on life, my relationship with God and my relationships with the people around me.

Just like John 1:12 says, it's like finding your true self.

But I'll be honest and admit that it wasn't something that happened overnight.

For me, it was more like a journey. Along the road, we've learned some lessons that I'd like to share with you today that will hopefully help you on your own journey to finding your true identity.

Along the Way, Here's What We Learned

The heavenly Father is perfect.

Yeah, right, 'Des, Duh!! We all know God is perfect, the Bible says so.

But let's take this point one step further and say:

God is perfect—therefore, he is not carrying a truckload of garbage around with him.

You see, the number one hinderance for most of us in developing our Father/child relationship with God is the imperfect parent/child relationships we've had in the past. I'm not saying it's always fathers, because many struggle with moms or grandparents or teachers or aunts or uncles or other adults in authority.

The point is that it isn't necessarily about *who* but it's about the fact that we hear that God wants to be our Father and we translate that phrase through the filter of the difficult relationship we've had with imperfect people in our lives.

I know I did. I heard "Father God" and thought "He must be as displeased and disappointed in me as my dad is ... nothing I do will ever be good enough or right enough and I'll spend my life trying to earn his love and never get it."

But what I learned on my journey was that God is perfect.

That means he's not carrying around all of the pain, anger, and abuse that my dad had in his heart and mind. He's not reacting to me out of pain like my dad did—rather he is

Chapter 9 ~ Finding Your Identity as a Child of God

always responding to me from his steady heart of love, compassion, grace, and purity.

I've learned that God the Father is not anything like your abuser.

He's never had a hateful, impure, inappropriate, jealous, manipulative, lying thought in his mind or committed a sinful action.

Deuteronomy 32:4 says, **"He is the Rock, his works are perfect, and all his ways are just. A faithful God who does no wrong, upright and just is he."**

2 Samuel 22:31 says, **"As for God, his way is perfect."**

When we truly allow this lesson to pierce through to our hearts, it is a game changer.

Rather than being afraid or approaching God with caution, we can finally come to him knowing that we are safe. There's nothing to be afraid of. He is a good Father and we can trust him to always be good and always be perfect.

Hebrews 4:16 (KJV) says, **"Let us therefore come boldly unto the throne of grace, that we may obtain mercy, and find grace to help in time of need."**

> *God is perfect. He is always responding to you from his steady heart of love, compassion, grace, and purity. God is not anything like your abuser.*

The heavenly Father is a loving Father.

So this point is definitely one of those points that can start to sound like Charlie Brown's teacher, "Blah, Blah, Blah, Blah, Blah."

We all know God loves us . . . we hear it all the time. God is love—that means he has to love everybody.

But if we are really going to truly grasp hold of what it means to be a child of God and have a healthy relationship with him, we're going to have to push a little further and realize that this point really is more than just "God loves you because he has to love you."

The truth is that God is absolutely crazy about you—as an individual.

> *God doesn't just love you because he's God and he has to—he actually likes you.*

He doesn't just love you because he's God and he has to—he actually likes you.

I remember the day when this truth really began to hit home in my heart and mind.

It was many years ago and there was a popular song that seemed to be absolutely everywhere. It would play in the grocery store, the department store, on commercials—you just couldn't get away from it. Right up front let me say that I know nothing about the artist or any of her music and I'm not endorsing it at all. It was just one of those songs that was everywhere.

Basically, the song was about a girl whose boyfriend told her everything that was wrong with her. She was stupid, she was useless, she couldn't do anything right. However, my an-

Chapter 9 — Finding Your Identity as a Child of God

tenna, always tuned into any form of music available, plugged into this song and started thinking about my relationship with my dad and how he'd made me feel this way over the years.

But then the song takes a turn, the drums bang and the electric guitar picked up and the singer belted out, **"But according to him—"** and then she listed all the ways that a different guy saw her and how knowing the other guy made her think that she was worth more than what she was settling for with her boyfriend.

In that moment, the Holy Spirit spoke to my heart and said:

"According to your dad you may be all of these bad things ... but according to your heavenly Father, all of those traits that your dad sees as negative are positives.

"They are the things that make your heavenly Father look at you and beam with pride.

"They are the qualities he put into your personality when you were born, because he had a plan and a purpose to use those characteristics exactly the way they are to make a difference in his kingdom.

"According to your heavenly Father you are loved, adored, wanted, enjoyed, appreciated—it's time to start seeing yourself according to him."

Now understand—I'm not having devotions while this is going on—I'm out of the house. The Holy Spirit's doing this major work in my heart and I'm a mess. But those words changed my heart.

Even though I understood from all the years of counseling I'd gone through when I first came home from college that my issues came from my dad's problems, his accusations weren't legitimate, and I needed to overcome, now I was finally realizing God sees me so much differently than I see myself.

He designed me with a purpose and a plan in mind.

Sure, there were parts of me that needed to be refined for his purposes, but God's goal was to do just that—take what he'd created and not destroy it, but make it better, stronger, more developed into the material that he could use to build his kingdom.

For the first time ever I was really able to grasp the fact that God the Father created me the way I am and LIKES me that way.

From that moment on, this truth changed my life because it set me free to be myself and even, dare I say, like myself.

Knowing that God really truly loved me and liked me just the way I was with all of my imperfections and idiosyncrasies—set me free to, as it says in John 12:1, find my true self and know that my true self was deeply and passionately loved by my heavenly Father.

Finally, I was able to truly grasp the meaning of verses like Psalm 147:11 that say, **"The LORD delights in those who fear him, who put their hope in his unfailing love."**

The truth is that God doesn't just tolerate you or put up with you—he truly from the depths of his heart loves you

> God truly from the depths of his heart loves you and wants what is best for you. You can trust that love and because of that, you can trust your relationship with him.

and wants what is best for you. You can trust that love and because of that, you can trust your relationship with him.

The heavenly Father is trustworthy.

This is another area that is very difficult for many of us to overcome in learning to be a daughter. I mean, if the word "father" makes us nervous, than the word "trust" can give us a panic attack. I know this has been true for me for a long time.

Again, my issues went back to the fact that I struggled to believe that the heavenly Father was trustworthy because my earthly dad was not.

Growing up, I learned at a very early age that the only thing I could really rely on Dad for was to do what was best for him. When there was an issue that had to be resolved, he would usually take the other person's side and leave my mom or brother or me hanging so that the other person wouldn't think badly of him. Even though I could always count on Mom to defend us, when it came to Dad, I knew I was on my own.

When my dad's secrets were ultimately revealed and we found out that he had serious issues with lying throughout our lives, it rocked our ability to trust.

All of these things combined with other areas of Dad's abuse left me having a very difficult time trusting God, relying on him to come through for me, and honestly, with the idea that I had to take care of myself and provide for myself.

Thankfully, God, in his loving concern for my spiritual and emotional well-being even more than my physical well-being, didn't want me to go through life being handicapped by the damage my father had caused. He placed me in situations where I had to learn to rely on him to provide.

Keeping it real, this was HARD!! There were times when my "walk of faith" resembled more of a struggle for me to let go of control and trust that God would take care of things while I held my breath and breathed into a bag.

But I can honestly stand before you today and say that throughout my journey I have learned that my heavenly Father is trustworthy.

I don't just believe that "My God shall supply all of my needs" because I learned this verse in Sunday School, but I believe it and know it to be true because I've seen God miraculously provide in situations that there was just absolutely no other way but him. I've seen him not only provide what was necessary but even what was beyond necessary and in every miracle I've learned that I can count on him.

Obviously, I'm not negating the necessity for financial responsibility and hard work, because these things are important. But what I've learned is that after I've done all that I can do and been as faithful as I can be with our finances, I can trust my heavenly Father to step in and provide because he is trustworthy.

Even more, along my journey I've learned that beyond finances I can trust God to do what is best for me.

I've learned that God is on the side of his children.

As Scripture says, he is working together all things for the good of those who love him and are called according to his purpose (Romans 8:28).

As I said, this has been a journey for me, and continues to be a journey.

This last point isn't really something that I learned in the distant past of my twenties, but more recently I found myself

Chapter 9 ～ Finding Your Identity as a Child of God

in a situation where someone was coming against us and I simply did not see a way out. I'd taken an honest look at the situation and even discussed it with a few close friends and we truly did not see where we had done anything wrong other than being deceived by someone who put up a really good front before revealing their true colors.

Suddenly we were faced with a situation that had the potential at the least to lose a significant amount of money, and at the worst, I feared what a lying tongue could do to my reputation, which as a minister is pretty important.

For literally months we prayed about this situation, and then it got worse. I didn't know what I was going to do.

Even though there were only a handful of people who knew the situation, I remember one godly woman saying, **"You are a child of God ... God is your Father ... and he will take care of this."**

As she prayed a powerful prayer, I just cried.

I remember later on being alone in my room in prayer, just laying it all out before God and saying:

"I honestly do not know what to do. I don't know how to fix this and I don't see anyway that you can fix this.

"But what I do know is that I can trust you.

"I know that you are perfect

"I know that you love me.

"I know that even if the worst happens, you are trustworthy and you will bring something good from this situation.

"So I leave this whole situation in your hands and trust that you are my Father and you will do what is best."

Trusting in my Father, I truly laid everything at the altar believing and hoping that he was trustworthy.

I wish I could say that I got up from that prayer and everything was better.

Instead, six weeks passed and then the phone rang.

In a way that only God could arrange, the issue was resolved. Someone who had no idea the problem existed made a seemingly unrelated decision that eliminated the problem. Suddenly we were protected and placed in a position where no weapon formed against us would prosper and no wagging tongue could stand. Even financially, we did not lose the money I thought was gone.

Besides just feeling shocked and awed, in that moment the most overwhelming thing that I felt was *loved*.

Protected.

Provided for.

I felt so safe in the arms of my heavenly Father who came to my rescue, provided my need, and delivered me from an enemy who wanted to cause destruction.

Friends, that's our heavenly Father.

He is a good Father that we can trust.

He is there for us and wants to come to our rescue.

He wants to be our provider, our protector, and our guide through life.

He wants what is best for us and works all things together for the good of his daughters so that we can fulfill his purpose in his kingdom.

After years of trusting him with my life, my heart, and my mind, I can testify to you today that you can trust him.

Like he did in our lives, he wants to heal the deepest issues of your heart and set you free from all that is holding you captive.

Chapter 9 ~ Finding Your Identity as a Child of God

Over twenty years ago, when I held my breath and said, "Yes, I'll do things your way" in the park, I had no idea what was coming. Yet, looking back now I can see that **every single thing** God allowed and did in our lives was for my good.

Today, neither Jamie or I are bound in the chains of perfection, the knots of pleasing people or earning love, secrets, abuse, lies, or shame.

We know that our value and identity come from God and him alone.

Our hearts no longer hurt and we are able to follow the calling God has for our unique lives.

God's even given us the strength to forgive our dad, to understand where he came from and to show him God's love. Today our dad lives with us. Even though the situation isn't always perfect, I believe the Holy Spirit is at work in his heart.

Having found our identity and significance in Jesus, realizing how deeply I am loved by my heavenly Father, and knowing that he smiles from ear to ear and is proud of me just because I am his daughter, I am now able to let my dad be who he is and find everything I need in Jesus.

Today, if you are still on the fence, tottering between "I know I need God to heal me and set me free" and "Can I trust him?" please let me encourage you to take the leap, trust God, and allow him to do a work of healing and deliverance in your life.

Start your journey.

Begin by applying the principles that we're going to talk about in the second half of this book and open the door to healing and wholeness in your own life.

Take the first step toward obtaining your own abundant life.

Trust your loving heavenly Father to do what is best for you and bring you into the life he's always dreamed for you.

Part 2:

The Journey to Healing

Chapter 10

Allowing the Holy Spirit Freedom to Work

Many books have been written on the topic of emotional and spiritual healing. I've read many of them throughout my life. Yet, very few, if any, talk about this very necessary ingredient: **Allowing the Holy Spirit the freedom to move and work in your life.**

Still, I know beyond a shadow of a doubt, that it was only through the active work of the Holy Spirit in our family that we were able to begin our journey, survive the pain, and ultimately find healing on the other side. Even though from the outside our lives looked bizarre and made absolutely no sense, behind closed doors the Holy Spirit was moving every day in the lives of our small family, moving mountains that only he could move and changing us into whom he wanted us to be.

You see, looking back I can see that it was the Holy Spirit putting the desire in our hearts that there had to be more to life than the "perfect charade" we were living, and leading my mom, Jamie, and me to ask God for more.

He was the one bringing my dad's suppressed memories to the surface.

He orchestrated the discovery of each secret and lie, and helped us see truth even in the darkest and most chaotic of situations.

It was his voice speaking words of life into our hearts and telling us which direction to go next.

In every step, he was convicting us of sin, leading us to repent, and make major changes in our lives.

Over and over again, like a beacon, he shined the light of truth helping us see that what was "normal" to us was completely abnormal. Through the Scriptures, he'd then help us find our way.

Through the hardest, most hellish of days, he was our comforter, our peace, and our strength.

It was the Holy Spirit that gave us the hope and the courage to keep persevering and moving on. Using both very natural and miraculously supernatural means, the Holy Spirit was our guide through our journey to healing. Without him, I'm sure we would not have survived.

That's why I believe that the first practical step each of us needs to make on our own personal journey to healing is deciding to give the Holy Spirit permission to work in our lives as he sees necessary.

Now I know—to many, this point can seem a little scary.

Yet I believe that the fear comes from not understanding who the Holy Spirit is and the role he is to play in the life of a believer.

For too long, the Holy Spirit has been seen as the odd man out in the Trinity.

I mean, we understand God the Father. Jesus came to earth to die for our sins and rose again. But the Holy Spirit

Chapter 10 — Allowing the Holy Spirit Freedom to Work

gets treated like the embarrassing black sheep in the family who makes people speak in strange tongues, faint in church, and get so excited they do everything but swing from the chandeliers.

While I completely believe in the Pentecostal doctrine, am baptized in the Holy Spirit, speak in tongues, and have seen the Holy Spirit move in supernatural ways, I think it's important that we understand that there is more to the Holy Spirit's identity and character that is often left unexplored. It is when we abandon our preconceived, stereotypical ideas about the Holy Spirit and give him free rein to fulfill God's will in our lives, that's when we begin to understand there is nothing to fear.

Perhaps the best place to begin this discussion is by answering the question:

Who is the Holy Spirit?

Simply put, the Holy Spirit is the third member of the Godhead or Trinity.

The Trinity consists of God the Father, Jesus the Son, and the Holy Spirit. As such, he has all the attributes of Deity in that he is eternal, unchanging, all-powerful, present everywhere, and has all knowledge.

As we study the Bible, we can see that he played an active role throughout, from Genesis 1:2 where he was involved in the creation of the world, straight through to Revelation as he guided John's writings. Even though he made appearances throughout the Old Testament, we really get to know him as Jesus introduces him in the New Testament.

In John 16, Jesus teaches his disciples about the Holy Spirit. He knew that the time for him to be crucified was quickly approaching, and he wanted them to know that even after he was gone they would not be alone.

"But very truly I tell you, it is for your good that I am going away. Unless I go away, the Advocate will not come to you; but if I go, I will send him to you. When he comes, he will prove the world to be in the wrong about sin and righteousness and judgment: about sin, because people do not believe in me; about righteousness, because I am going to the Father, where you can see me no longer; and about judgment, because the prince of this world now stands condemned.

"I have much more to say to you, more than you can now bear. But when he, the Spirit of truth, comes, he will guide you into all the truth. He will not speak on his own; he will speak only what he hears, and he will tell you what is yet to come. He will glorify me because it is from me that he will receive what he will make known to you. All that belongs to the Father is mine. That is why I said the Spirit will receive from me what he will make known to you (John 16:7–15).

As you read these verses, it's important to know the background.

> When we abandon our preconceived, stereotypical ideas about the Holy Spirit and give him free rein to fulfill God's will in our lives, we begin to understand that there is nothing to fear.

Chapter 10 — Allowing the Holy Spirit Freedom to Work

Essentially, Jesus is preparing his disciples for what's to come. He knows what's coming—he's going to be taken prisoner, crucified, and die. Even after he rises from the dead, he isn't going to stay with them forever—no, his work is completed at the cross and he is going back to heaven.

Still, he wants them to know that they aren't going to be left alone. Instead, the Holy Spirit is coming after him to help them. Rather than being "with them," the Holy Spirit will be "inside of them," leading, guiding, and empowering them as they live their lives and do the work God wants them to do.

That's why he said it is better for them that the Holy Spirit comes.

The good news for us is that the powerful work of the Holy Spirit didn't end at the close of New Testament times. The same Holy Spirit who was present at creation, worked throughout the Old Testament, filled Jesus, and anointed and guided the early church, wants to be equally active in our lives today. Allowing him to play a living, vibrant, active role in your day-to-day life is the key to living a Spirit-led life.

> *The same Holy Spirit who was present at creation, worked throughout the Old Testament, filled Jesus, and anointed and guided the early church wants to be equally active in our lives today.*

Let's look at a few of the ways the Holy Spirit wants to actively influence your life.

The Holy Spirit convicts us of sin.

"When he comes, he will prove the world to be in the wrong about sin and righteousness and judgment" (John 16:8).

One of the Holy Spirit's main functions is convicting people of sin. Rather than seeing this as a bad thing, we need to see this as an exciting opportunity to change, become more Christ-like, and deepen our relationship with God.

The truth is that all of us have different areas in our lives that we need to overcome and replace God's ways where there are sinful patterns. We are all in the process of separating from sin and evil and dedicating ourselves to the worship and service of Christ. This process is called sanctification.

Throughout our story, there were many times when the Holy Spirit played this role in our lives. Often times convicting us of things that we didn't even see as sin or we'd found ways to conveniently excuse, he would shine his light of conviction and show us not only how gross that sin was in God's eyes, but how much pain and destruction it was causing.

When the Holy Spirit convicts us of sin, he is challenging us to take another step forward in this process.

Conviction says, **"This sin is providing an obstacle in your relationship with God and a barrier to you becoming all God wants you to be. It's time to repent, abandon this sin, and form a new behavioral pattern following the principles of the Bible."**

Conviction is like a WRONG WAY sign. Its sole purpose is to make you aware that you are going in the wrong direction so you can turn around and get back on course. The benefit of living a Spirit-led life and heeding the Holy Spirit's voice of conviction is that he will make you aware of sin so you can make adjustments and get on the right spiritual path.

Heeding the voice of the Holy Spirit when he convicts you of sin should be an on-going process in the life of every believer. It is our duty to keep our spiritual ears open and our hearts sensitive so we can experience the conviction of the Holy Spirit and quickly respond in repentance and change. As we grow closer to God and live a more Spirit-led life, sensing and responding to the conviction of the Holy Spirit will become a common occurrence as he leads you into a holier, more sanctified, more intimate relationship with Jesus. What an awesome gift!

The Holy Spirit guides us into all truth.

"But when he, the Spirit of truth, comes, he will guide you into all the truth" (John 16:13).

Reading through our story, you know that we needed to be guided into truth because we were genuinely deceived. There were so many areas of life that we thought were right, normal, and even godly that were just completely twisted and wrong. Without the Holy Spirit stepping into each of these situations and saying, *"This is truth and this is lies,"* we would have never started, let alone finished, our journey to healing.

The good news is that he wants to play this role in the life of every believer.

We live in a world where it is hard to know what is true and what is false. Deception runs rampant through families, through society, and sometimes even throughout the church.

How can a Christian know what is true and what is a lie?

By relying on the Holy Spirit.

One way the Holy Spirit leads us into truth is by giving us the gift of discernment. Using this spiritual gift, we will be able to judge right from wrong, truth from lies, and the things of God versus cheap imitations.

Another common way that the Holy Spirit leads us into truth is by helping us to better understand the Bible and apply it to our own lives. Under his guidance, the words of the Bible become a living word for each of us. As we study the teaching of Jesus, the Holy Spirit gives us insight into their meaning.

How can a Christian know what is true and what is a lie? By relying on the Holy Spirit.

The NIV Disciple Study Bible says, "The Spirit is present at the Christian's study desk and in every Christian study group, leading believers into all truth."[1]

The Holy Spirit guides believers.

How can Christians know which direction God wants them to go and what he wants them to do?

The answer is by living lives that are led by the Holy Spirit.

Acts 20:22–24 records Paul's statements to the Ephesian elders explaining how he knew it was God's will for him to go to Jerusalem:

> **"And now, compelled by the Spirit, I am going to Jerusalem, not knowing what will happen to me there. I only know that in every city the Holy**

Spirit warns me that prison and hardships are facing me. However, I consider my life worth nothing to me; my only aim is to finish the race and complete the task the Lord Jesus has given me—the task of testifying to the good news of God's grace."

Just as Paul knew God's will because of the guidance of the Holy Spirit, Christians today can learn God's will through the guidance of the Holy Spirit.

Romans 8:14 (ESV) says, **"For all who are led by the Spirit of God are sons of God."**

The same Holy Spirit that told Paul to go to Jerusalem wants to direct your steps everyday of your life. He wants to be *your* guide, the GPS for *your* life. He wants to develop a relationship with you that allows him to speak to your heart and give you direction.

There are many more roles that the Holy Spirit fills in the life of believers.

He gives joy.

He teaches.

He testifies of Christ.

He strengthens and encourages.

He enables us to endure persecution.

He comforts us and helps us in our weakness.

He intercedes for us.

He sanctifies.

He imparts the gifts of the Spirit, and he develops the Christ-like character of the fruit of the Spirit in our lives.

Those who are serious about overcoming the issues in the past, the pain in their hearts, and the sin in their lives NEED the Holy Spirit to fulfill every one of these tasks in their lives.

So let's get practical.

So we've talked about who the Holy Spirit is and why we need him to be at work in our lives. Now let's talk about some practical ways that we can welcome him into our healing process.

1. Don't close the door.

If you are feeling a nudge in your spirit to overcome areas in your life, forgive the past, find healing, or start new behavioral patterns, the truth is that you're already experiencing the work of the Holy Spirit. He is the one calling you, nudging your heart saying, "There's more to life than the pain you're living in. Come and find the abundant life Jesus has for you."

Now it's decision time for you: Are you going to answer his call or close the door and reject his invitation?

2. Listen for his voice.

As you're going through the healing process, it's important that you allow the Holy Spirit to speak to your heart.

Okay, I know, this is where some people panic and say, *"What does that mean? I'm going to hear voices from heaven? Yeah, now we're getting a little to strange for me."*

First, calm down. The truth is that even though the Holy Spirit has played a very active role in our lives, I have never actually heard an audible voice from out of nowhere saying, "Do this." (Trust me, I'd be freaked out, too!)

While I'm not saying it's impossible, it is far more common that the Holy Spirit will speak to us from God's Word. As you're praying, God will bring a verse to your mind that will speak to your situation or you'll be reading Scripture and it will almost jump off the page as you know it pertains to your need.

I cannot tell you how many times this happened to us as we were going through the healing process. At just the right time, the Holy Spirit would lead us to a verse that would convict of sin, provide God's truth, guide us, or provide comfort. As we studied and meditated on those Scriptures, we knew the next steps to take on our journey to healing.

Another way the Holy Spirit speaks to people is by putting thoughts into their minds as they pray. Again, this is something we've experienced many times. Often it was like a light bulb of truth went off inside my brain helping me see something differently than I'd ever seen it before. Sometimes it was just a word or phrase; other times the Holy Spirit spoke so much and the words flowed so freely that we actually wrote them down as if the Holy Spirit was writing a letter.

For instance, I've often told the story of the day when the Holy Spirit spoke the truth into my mind that even though there were many things my dad didn't like about me, those were the things that God placed inside of me when I was born and he loved those things.

Did I hear an audible voice that day? No.

Yet I know from years of having the Holy Spirit speak to my heart that those thoughts came from him.

How do you know if it's the Holy Spirit speaking to you?

Most people ask themselves this question when they are first learning to hear the voice of the Holy Spirit.

One test is to ask yourself: **Does what I believe I've heard line up with Scripture?**

The Holy Spirit will NEVER go against the Bible. In fact, almost every time the Holy Spirit speaks to you, he will confirm it with Scripture. So when it doubt, ask yourself, "Does this agree with Scripture?"

Another test is to look for confirmation.

I cannot tell you how many times the Holy Spirit would confirm his words to us through Scripture, through sermons, through other people, or even through coincidences. Often as we were going through our healing process, trying to sort out lies from truth, the Holy Spirit would actually back up the words he'd speak to us in private with concrete confirmation that what he'd spoken was true.

There is nothing wrong with looking for these confirmations—especially when you're just beginning to recognize the voice of the Holy Spirit. Trust me, the Holy Spirit wants you to learn to hear and obey his voice, so he will provide confirmations so that you'll be assured it is his voice and you need to obey.

One final thing that we did when we were first learning to follow the Holy Spirit was to ask Spirit-filled, godly leaders to help us discern whether or not we were hearing God. We asked several pastors—I even asked my theology professor at college, *"Is it possible that the Holy Spirit could be speaking in this way and saying this?"*

There is no shame in asking for help. There's actually biblical precedent.

In 1 Samuel, Samuel did not recognize the voice of the Lord calling to him until Eli explained to him what was happening and how to respond. There is nothing wrong with finding a spiritual mentor who will help you learn to hear and respond properly to the voice of the Holy Spirit. Just make sure that you go to someone who is baptized in the Holy Spirit and who knows how to hear the voice of God themselves. Anyone who is already on this road will be glad to help you learn to live a Spirit-led life.

Chapter 10 ~ Allowing the Holy Spirit Freedom to Work

The most important part of this process is that once you know the Holy Spirit is speaking to you, you choose to obey him and do what he says.

This is a step that I see too many Christians ignore to their own detriment.

You see, it's an amazing thing to hear the Holy Spirit speak to your heart. It's a precious gift directly from heaven. Yet, often times, many people know what God wants them to do, but they reject it.

They put it off—make excuses—choose to take a different path.

The blunt reality is that those who take this path find themselves five, ten, fifteen years later in the same place, dealing with the same pain and defeated by the same problems. The irony is that they often blame the Holy Spirit for not working when it is really their fault for not obeying what he told them to do.

> *Find a spiritual mentor who will help you learn to hear and respond properly to the voice of the Holy Spirit.*

The Holy Spirit said, *"Remember"*; they said, *"No way."*
The Holy Spirit said, *"Forgive"*; they said *"Can't do it."*
The Holy Spirit said, *"Change"*; they said, *"Maybe someday but not now."*

By making these decisions and others like them, they are blocking the Holy Spirit from being able to work in their lives. Even though they may talk about healing and pray for healing, it is their own disobedience that keeps them from receiving healing and experiencing abundant life in Christ.

Looking back on our story, I saw two people take two different paths. Whenever the Holy Spirit offered a new level of healing to my mom, she always jumped at the opportunity, no matter the cost. On the other hand, my dad always chose to close the door. Even as we were on our journey to healing, this happened time and time again as my dad fought the Holy Spirit's work in trying to help him remember things, bringing healthy counselors into his life, or making life changes. Most of the chaos and pain that we lived through during this time was because, rather than agreeing with the Holy Spirit and going through the healing process willingly, my dad fought the Holy Spirit's work.

Having seen choices and experienced the consequences, my best advice is to allow the Holy Spirit to do whatever he wants to do in your heart. Fighting him is like a man with a broken arm using his healthy arm to keep the doctor who can set the injured bone away. You're hurting yourself, preventing your healing, and if you're successful in your attempt to keep the Holy Spirit away, you're the one who is going to have to live with the permanent pain and consequences of your choices. Don't do it!

Instead, listen to the warning in Hebrews: **"Today, if you hear his voice, do not harden your hearts"** (3:15).

If you hear the Holy Spirit calling you, answer his call with a resounding, "Yes!"

Give him the freedom to play an active role in your life and your healing, using every means available to help you overcome and be the person God has called you to be.

That's step one on the road to healing.

Chapter 11

Spending Time with Jesus

One of the biggest lies that we've bought into in modern day Christianity is that we can maintain a healthy, thriving relationship with Jesus by praying while we're doing other things. If we squeeze in a few minutes while we're driving in the car or pray while we're doing a chore, we've believe that's all we need.

Please don't think I'm saying it's wrong to pray throughout the day. Quite the contrary, the apostle Paul encourages us in 1 Thessalonians 5:17 to **"Pray continually."**

However, what we've learned on our journey is that if you are serious about pursuing personal freedom and healing from the things that are stealing life from you, it's going to take more than just a few minutes of prayer on the go here and there. Instead, you're going to have to consciously schedule significant periods of time to be alone with Jesus and work on the issues of your heart.

I know, I know. We're all busy.

Modern life is demanding and our days seem to fill up and time evaporates before we know it. Yet, there are times

Finding Healing

in life when you need to prioritize important things which may necessitate moving other things to the side.

For instance, recently a friend of mine had knee replacement surgery. After years of suffering in pain and dealing with mobility issues, the opportunity came for her to find some relief. She could hardly wait to get back to living with less pain and more mobility in her life.

The only thing was that even after the surgery was over, she could not get right back out and walk however and wherever she wanted. First, she had to go through a period of recovery that included going to physical therapy several times a week.

During this time, physical therapy became the top priority in her life. Even though there were many other things she would have liked to be doing with her days or even things that needed to be done, she set this time aside each day to drive to therapy, go through the routine, drive home, and continue doing her exercises because she knew that it was only through making this commitment that her knee would properly heal and she'd be able to get on back to the full life she desired.

So what does this have to do with spending time with Jesus?

Well, just like my friend had to make a commitment and set aside time to go to physical therapy so that her knee could heal properly, whenever we are serious about pursuing healing for our hearts and minds, we need to make spending time with Jesus our top priority. It's like physical therapy for our hearts and minds. It doesn't matter if we think we're too busy or we don't have time—if we want to actively pursue healing we are going to have to make the time to be alone with Jesus so he can heal our hearts.

This was a commitment that each of us had to make individually throughout our journey. Usually for me, it meant setting aside a specific time during the day, going to my room, shutting the door, and entering into prayer. Obviously, for each person the time and place will be different because the schedules and demands of our lives are different. What's important is that you find a time that works for you. While one person may find early morning the quietest, most peaceful option, another person may find that the busiest time in their daily routine and choose to set aside time at night or during the day. The important thing isn't necessarily when—it's that you do it.

Just like we would look at our schedule before we'd set up a physical therapy routine and say, *"This is when I can realistically make this commitment happen on a consistent basis,"* we need to look at our schedule and say, *"This is when I am going to schedule uninterrupted time with Jesus."* Then block it on your calendar, your phone, or however you track your time and commit to consistently keeping this appointment.

One of the next questions that many people ask whenever we talk about a commitment to spending time with Jesus is, **"Okay, once I've set aside a specific amount of time, what am I going to do with it?"**

Because, let's be honest, if you're haven't already developed the spiritual discipline of prayer, the concept of spending a specific block of time in prayer can seem daunting.

Let's start off by saying what this type of prayer is not.

When you've set aside a specific amount of time to allowing Jesus to work on this issues of your heart, this is not the time to take your prayer list and start praying for everyone that you know. This isn't the time to intercede for lost loved ones, pray for every missionary that came to your church, or every person that you know has a physical need.

Those are all prayers of intercession. While there is a time for intercessory prayer and being an intercessor is an admirable calling, this is not the type of prayer that will help you on your pursuit to freedom and healing. Sometimes, God will call us to set this type of prayer aside so that we can focus on finding healing.

Don't stress about this. It's okay. There is a time and a place for everything. While you're going through a time of healing, God will call someone else to a time of intercessory prayer. Just like my friend isn't going to spend the rest of her life in physical therapy for her knee, if you allow the Holy Spirit to heal the wounds in your heart and bring you healing, there will come a day when you won't have to focus so much of your prayer time on healing. Then God may call you to intercession while he calls someone else to a time of healing.

> You're going to have to consciously schedule significant periods of time to be alone with Jesus and work on the issues of your heart.

What's important is that while the Holy Spirit is calling you to this time of inner healing, you answer his call and allow him to do the work in your heart and mind that can only happen as you spend time alone with Jesus working on the issues of your heart.

This brings us once again to the question of **"What should I talk to God about?"**

The answer is simple: the needs of your own heart, soul, and mind.

"But what does that look like?? What exactly am I supposed to do??"

To answer that question, all I can do is tell you what it looked like for me—and it looked different depending on what we were going through at the time.

Looking back, I remember there were days when it wasn't hard at all to know what to talk to Jesus about when I went to pray. The morning after we'd gone through a night where my dad had one of his tantrums, or a secret had just been uncovered, or something had been said that broke my heart, it was easy to go into my room, lock the door, and just pour our my heart to Jesus telling him everything that I thought, felt, hated, wanted, and needed at the time.

There was just so much emotion. Having nowhere else to go with the hurt, pain, confusion, and anger, I would just go to my room and just unload it all at Jesus' feet. Sometimes there'd be tears, other times, anger. When my heart was overwhelmed, I'd go to Jesus and say, "Where do we go from here?"

As we're going through the process of healing, it's important that we understand that it's not a sin to do this. In fact, the Bible encourages it.

Psalm 62:8 (ESV) says, **"Trust in him at all times, O people; pour out your heart before him; God is a refuge for us."**

As we look at the great men and women of the Bible we see them often going to God and telling him every single thing that they thought and felt—the good, the bad, and the downright ugly.

Don't believe me? Take a look at the Psalms, the book of Job, or the book of Jeremiah. Notice that even though these words were written by some of God's greatest, most righteous men, they had some powerful thoughts and feelings that they brought before God. Yet, God never turned away from them or rejected their honesty. Instead, he met them where they were and helped them overcome, heal, and grow even deeper in their relationship with him.

Looking back on some of the conversations I've had with God, I have to admit that I'm really glad he was the only one listening. I'm very sure that if I'd have said some of the things I said to him to a person, they'd have condemned me as a backslidden sinner. Yet, God never did.

Why?

Well, first of all because he wasn't shocked. Psalm 139 makes it pretty clear that God knows every thought that goes through our minds. So even before you say something to him in prayer, he already knows you're thinking it.

God doesn't just know our thoughts and feelings. He also knows what caused them. He also knows WHY we think and feel the way we do—often times to a greater extent than we do. That's what he can show us as we spend time with him in prayer.

You see, many times we go to God saying, "This hurts so badly—fix it."

> *As we spend time with Jesus, he can take us back to the very origin of our pain and show us what is necessary to remember, to forgive, to overcome, and to heal.*

In his eternal wisdom God says, "I know it hurts, but in order to fix it, I'm going to have to fix you."

As we cooperate, the Holy Spirit can then show us the REAL source of our pain—the trigger. Often it's completely different than we think because we don't really understand the deepest wounds of our hearts. But as we spend time with Jesus, being completely honest and open with him, he can take us back to the very origin of our pain and show us what is necessary to remember, to forgive, to overcome, and to heal.

We've seen it happen over and over again as individuals and as a family. We have journals filled with the stories of days when we kept our appointment with Jesus, thinking we'd talk about one thing only to have the Holy Spirit use that trigger to completely heal another. On a completely ordinary day when we thought we were just going to pray, our lives changed forever. That's the reward of spending time with Jesus.

Of course, not every day is an emotionally overwhelming day. (Thank God for that!)

What do you do on those days?

On the days when you aren't in crisis mode, it's still very important to keep your appointment with Jesus. (Just like my friend kept her physical therapy appointments on the days her leg felt better and on the days her leg felt bad.)

One thing that I recommend on these days to help get your prayer time focused is to begin with worship.

Nothing helps you enter God's presence like worship.

Psalm 100:4 says, **"Enter his gates with thanksgiving and his courts with praise!"**

Why start your time of prayer with worship?

Basically, because worship changes your focus.

As you sing or listen to praise and worship music, you begin focusing on the greatness of God, the wonders of his love, his power, and his sovereignty. Your mindset shifts from all the challenges in your life and moves toward his sovereignty, his control, and his ability to lead and direct your paths.

Worship reminds us that we are small and he is great. As our normally self-centered minds adjust to this proper repositioning and realignment, we can't help but be overwhelmed by his immense love for us, that one so great would care about us and call us his children. It's in these moments that the "stuff of earth" fades away, opening up our heart to talk to our heavenly Father.

Sometimes worship means listening to praise and worship music. Other times it means singing your own worship songs.

Personally, I do different variations of all of these things from time to time, although my mind does tend to wander less when I'm singing rather than listening, but that's me. It isn't really the method or even quality of the sound of music that matters. What I've found is that whenever I open my time of prayer with a time of worship, my perspective changes and open, heart-felt communication quickly follows.

Another thing that often helps me enter into the presence of God and prepare my heart for honest communication is spending a few minutes praying in my prayer language (more commonly called speaking in tongues). When I release control, stop trying to come up with things to say, and allow the Holy Spirit to pray through me, I often find that this gives the Holy Spirit the freedom to then lead my mind in the direction he wants to guide our time together that day. Because he knows what is broken and needs healing much better than I do, I've often found that this practice leads to some of the best times of prayer in my life.

Being completely vulnerable, I will admit that whenever I enter into a time of personal, private worship, it almost immediately and spontaneously leads me into a time of confession. How could it not?

Think about it: Worship leads you into the presence of God.

God is absolute holiness.

It's usually during this time that the Holy Spirit reminds me of words I shouldn't have spoken, something I shouldn't have watched, or an attitude in my heart that doesn't belong. That's how worship almost seamlessly leads to confession, as I take this time to repent and ask God to forgive me for the things in my life that are offensive to him—the things that don't belong there. Quite frankly, many of these things are things that I am somehow calloused to until I enter into God's presence.

In Psalms 51:10, King David prayed, **"Create in me a clean heart, O God; and renew a right spirit within me."**

I'll be honest and admit that often my time of confession goes beyond simply confessing things I've done wrong, and into talking openly with God about things that are wrong inside of me. Let me give you an example. (But keep it to yourself, this is personal.)

I remember a day when I started off my time of prayer listening to some worship music. Soon, I found myself confessing the sin of being really short tempered in my conversation with a family member. However, the conversation didn't end with me telling God I was sorry. Instead, I started pouring out my heart to God about some things this person did that were very hurtful to me, and how this person's choices were creating a poison in my heart and were triggering my short temper.

As the conversation of prayer continued, the Holy Spirit began helping me deal with the real issues of my heart, showing me things from a different perspective, and challenging me to make different choices that didn't allow the poison into my heart that was causing me to sin.

Rather than these moments being simply a recitation of things I needed to repent of, this time became a "healing session" as the Holy Spirit dealt with the root of my problem and began the process of "creating a right spirit within me."

The truth is that often our pain or the damage in our soul causes us to sin. It could be a wrong attitude, a wrong behavior, or sometimes just downright rebellion against God. As we confess those sins, the Holy Spirit is able to point out what's causing us to sin and continue the healing process in our hearts.

That's why I believe that this time of confession involves not only confessing the sins we've committed that have offended God, but also talking with God about the people and situations in our lives that have offended us.

In Luke 11:4, we see that Jesus includes both angles when he teaches his disciples how to pray: **"Forgive us our sins, for we also forgive everyone who sins against us."**

Here's a tool that we've found to be tremendously helpful in our times of both confessing our sins and in dealing with the pain of those who've sinned against us.

Are you ready?

It's really old fashioned, but it helps:

I make lists.

I told you it was old-fashioned, but sometimes the old ways are best.

Many, many times as I was going through this time of healing, my time locked away with Jesus would be spent with pen and paper in hand, making lists.

For instance, I remember when the Holy Spirit was convicting us of following in our dad's footsteps of lying, the Holy Spirit asked me to a make list of every single time I could remember ever lying, then go back through the list confessing those sins to God.

When I'd fallen into the trap of watching things on television that were borderline pornography, I remember making a list of every single program I watched that I shouldn't have and individually asking God to forgive me for each one.

As the lists were made, we were not only confessing sins, but we were able to see patterns develop.

When did we fall into these sins?

What was happening?

What were the triggers, the causes?

What were the real areas we needed to overcome?

Even though this practice may seem a little over the top or old fashioned, the truth is that it was powerful—so much more powerful than a blanket, "I'm sorry for every time I ever . . . ."

It helped me thoroughly confess my sin, see what needed to change, and what I needed to be healed from to help me change. Although few would call this standard "prayer," it was during our time with Jesus that these lists were made, sins were forgiven and overcome, and our hearts were healed.

Of course, I didn't just make lists of my sins. As I said, I also made lists of things that people had done to me.

For instance, I remember one time when I was seriously hurt by the words of someone close to the family. Without going into details, it's sufficient to say that someone close to our family chose that they did not want to know the truth about what was happening in our lives (they expressed this desire openly and verbally), yet they felt the need to share their opinion that it was all my fault. Even though we all knew this person's opinions were devoid of facts of truth, the words still hurt a lot.

Not knowing where to go with the pain, I went to Jesus. During my time of prayer, I felt the Holy Spirit leading me to make a list of every time this person had hurt me. As I made the list I realized that it wasn't just this one word causing the pain. There were many words or actions that needed to be forgiven that were causing years of backed up pain. As I took every item on the list and asked God to help me forgive the person, I was released from years of pain and knots from this person's misguided opinions.

Although the issue was never resolved with the other person (because they were not open to it), inside my heart the issue was resolved. I was able to walk away free from the pain and over time stop caring what this person thought of me. Through the help of the Holy Spirit, I was able to show God's love to someone who consistently treated me badly because I was no longer emotionally tied to them.

Again, that's the power that's available to us as we choose to daily spend time with Jesus!

Chapter 11 — Spending Time with Jesus

You see, what we learned in our own lives is that yes, life is busy. You can always find things to fill the time that should belong to Jesus—it's not even hard. In fact, sometimes it's really hard to reprioritize and sacrifice to schedule time with Jesus into your life and your day.

Yet, there is no other road to healing.

It is simply impossible to be healed of the deepest wounds in your heart, soul, and mind without spending time with your spiritual physician: Jesus.

Here's the other thing we've learned: After years of living life tied up in knots and carrying emotional pain that was keeping us from the abundant life Jesus had for us, the freedom was worth the investment of time.

Even more, having seen the example of our father who wasted far too many years of his life not letting Jesus heal the wounds in his heart, I believe that there really is no option. Like my friend who decided to have surgery and go through physical therapy, there comes a point where you to decide to stop living in debilitating pain and do what is necessary to heal.

What's necessary to heal is spending time with Jesus.

When your prayer life includes open and honest conversations with God about the real problems in your life—the relationship struggles, the issues in your mind and the heartaches in your soul—you're getting into some pretty intimate

> *It is simply impossible to be healed of the deepest wounds in your heart, soul, and mind without spending time with your spiritual physician: Jesus.*

territory. That's when prayer becomes a relationship and not just an appointment you have to keep.

As you begin to see the healing take place, it will become less of a chore and more of a joy as you experience the exceedingly full, rich life that true healing can bring.

Chapter 12

Soaking in God's Word

*L*ooking back on our journey to healing, I have to say that next to the commitment to spending time with Jesus, the next best decision that I made was to dig into the Word of God like never before so that it could heal the wounds in my heart.

Not that this was a new concept for me at all. The truth is that we'd grown up reading the Bible. Our mom loved the Bible and was passionate about Bible reading and Bible study throughout her life. Wanting to pass this desire on to Jamie and me, she taught us to read the Bible every day and even put it on our chore charts.

We also received a lot of Bible teaching in school where we had daily devotions, the Bible was taught in the curriculum, and we were required to memorize Scripture on a monthly basis. After high school, I went on to Bible college where the Bible was the main textbook in all of our learning. I read it, studied it, and even preached from it.

Still, it wasn't until after we graduated from Bible college that the Holy Spirit was really able to begin using the Bible to heal our hearts and reshape our minds. Perhaps it was because until then, we didn't know we had anything that needed to be fixed. After all, remember, we were "perfect."

After this illusion was blown to smithereens and there were no sermons to prepare, no one to impress with our exegesis skills, and I really needed answers for what was happening in my life, that's when I made the decision to really dig into God's Word and allow the Holy Spirit to change my heart.

My new goal was to find out:

What does God really want?

How does he really feel about me?

Can God's Word help me find truth among the lies, comfort among the pain, and untie all of the knots that were tying up my heart and soul?

As I committed to spending time in God's Word on a consistent basis, the Holy Spirit was faithful and used the Bible to help me find answers to these questions and many more.

Some of the ways that the Holy Spirit used the Word of God to heal my heart was through convicting me of sin, providing comfort in pain, strengthening me, and giving me courage through the difficult times through God's promises, and guiding me in the way I needed to go. However, looking back, I'd have to say one of the biggest ways he used the Bible was to expose truth.

John 8:32 says, **"Then you will know the truth, and the truth will set you free."**

John 17:17 (NLT) says, **"Make them holy by your truth; teach them your word, which is truth."**

2 Timothy 2:15 calls the Bible **the Word of Truth.**

Hence, the only way to find the truth that will set you free is through the Word of God.

Chapter 12 ⇾ Soaking in God's Word

As you know from reading our story, we needed to find the truth. You see, so many of our problems—the secrets, the abuse, the knots—they were all the result of lies. Not just lies that we were told, but lies that we believed . . . lies that were defining how we saw ourselves, how we saw God, and how we lived our lives.

It wasn't until the Holy Spirit started using God's Word to shine a bright light of truth into our lives that we were able to see that the things we thought were normal or even godly were far from what God wanted. They were man-made lies. It was the truth of God's Word that set us free.

For example, it was through studying the life of Jesus and how he interacted with people while he walked on earth that the Holy Spirit opened my eyes to God's true heart for women. As I studied passage by passage, I saw that Jesus' heart and actions were totally different than our dad had said was God's attitude toward women. Verse by verse, the Holy Spirit used this time of study to untie my knots and set me free.

The same was true for Jamie. As the Holy Spirit led him to study different men in the Bible, he began to truly understand God's definition of godly manhood and how God defined a strong man. With each man he studied, the Holy Spirit helped him see the difference between our dad's definition of manhood and God's. Seeing the truth, Jamie was set free to be the man God called him to be.

Just as Hebrews 4:12 said, the Holy Spirit used the Scriptures we were studying to cut through all of our thoughts and attitudes and get right to the heart of the matter. Seeing the truth, we were able to shake off the lies and begin to heal.

So let's get practical and talk about exactly how we can apply the Word of God as an ointment that heals the wounds in our hearts and minds.

One of the first things you can do is make a commitment to daily meditate on the Word of God.

Keep this Book of the Law always on your lips; meditate on it day and night, so that you may be careful to do everything written in it. Then you will be prosperous and successful (Joshua 1:8).

Over the years the word *meditate* has gotten a bad connotation as it's been connected to the practices of Eastern religions. Just to be clear, this is not the type of "meditating" we're talking about. Christians have no business practicing yoga!

Rather, in the Bible the word *meditate* means "mutter" or to say or think about it over and over again.

Rather than being strange or mystical, it's actually very practical.

Meditating means more than just speed reading or reading to get through it, but it means going over it in your mind—analyzing it, pondering it, thinking about it. You're actually pondering what it means to you so that you can apply it to your lives.

Rick Warren explains biblical meditation as "thought digestion."[1] God wants us to get every ounce of spiritual nutrition out of his Word. He wants us to chew on it, digest it, and then chew on it some more.

Practical ways that I found to do this are:

- *Slow down. Read shorter passages. Read slower. Read for comprehension; not words per minute.*

- *Try reading the same passage in several different versions. The Bible App or YouVersion make it really easy to click from version to version without having ten different Bibles on the table. Yet, by reading different versions you will pick up different inferences* or inflections. Because they use different words to explain the same thoughts, it will help your mind better comprehend the true meaning of a verse.

- Try reading it out loud.
- After you're read a passage, sit quietly for five minutes and think about what that passage means to you.
- If you really want to go all out, write down what you learn in a journal. Write down how the verse affected you, what you felt the Holy Spirit speaking to you through a verse, or how you can practically apply it to your life. The truth is that over the course of my journey to healing, I filled many journals with Scriptures that healed my heart and set me free. I still have many of those journals, reminding me of God's faithfulness and healing power.

> *The Scriptures cut through all of our thoughts and attitudes and got right to the heart of the matter. Seeing the truth, we were able to shake off the lies and begin to heal.*

Take advantage of helpful tools.

Sometimes as we're reading the Bible, we'll come across a passage that is difficult to understand. Perhaps a verse will stand out and we know the Holy Spirit wants to use it to change us, but we're just not quite sure what it really means in practical terms.

Thankfully, there are several resources available to help us more fully understand the Scriptures and apply them to our lives. Whenever I want to dive deeper into the Bible, and explore a verse's true meaning, the first thing I do is turn to a commentary.

Commentaries

What is a commentary? A commentary is a book written by scholars who have researched the ancient Hebrew and Greek, the history of the passage, and the original context of the passage to decipher what the Scripture truly means. Two of my favorite commentaries are: *Zondervan NIV Bible Commentary*[2] and *Barnes Notes on the New Testament*.[3] If you are just getting started, I would strongly recommend purchasing *Zondervan's NIV Bible Commentary* by Barker and Kohlenberger (Volume 1 & 2). This is a very thorough, easy-to-read, amazing commentary set and you will not regret the investment!

Want to dig even deeper into the meaning of a verse? How about trying a word study?

Trust me, it's not as difficult as it seems; in fact, it's kind of fun and very rewarding and helpful as you seek to understand Scripture.

How do you get started?

First, choose a word that seems important to the verse. (For example in James 1:3, you might choose *perseverance*.)

Next, look up the word *perseverance* in the English dictionary.

Bible translators have done an excellent job in translating the Bible from the original Greek or Hebrew. Often the reason we don't understand what the Bible is saying because we have a poor understanding of the true meaning of words in the English language. That's why the good old *Webster's Dictionary* is a good place to start.

What I found was that as I set aside time every day to not just read but also dig a little deeper and find the true meaning of a passage, my faith was growing. The Holy Spirit was using what I was learning to speak words of truth into my life, words of conviction, guidance, and healing. It was like a person who is struggling physically sitting down every day to a healthy meal—I was gaining spiritual nutrition, muscle, and strength. I was gaining health and freedom because I was ingesting God's Word and applying it to my life.

Topical Studies

Another very practical way that our family used the Word of God on our road to healing was to do topical studies and find out exactly what the Bible had to say about specific topics, struggles, and sins we were fighting to overcome.

For instance, when we found out about my dad's debt, together as a family we searched out and studied every verse in the Bible that talked about debt or money. (There are a lot!)

When I was struggling with fear, I studied what the Bible said about overcoming fear.

Honestly, the list of topical studies we did could go on forever because we implemented this practice into our lives whenever we faced a new area that we needed to overcome. For almost every chapter in this book (and many more) we did a topical study to find God's perspective and what changes we needed to make in our lives. Although this wasn't something I did every day, it was an important part of our journey to healing and gaining freedom from specific issues. Exactly how did we do it?

Back in the day, before we had computers and the Internet, we used *Strong's Concordance*[4] to find every place the Bible talked about a certain topic. Then with pen and paper in hand, we'd write it out and use commentaries to study it. We even went so far as to type out our notes so that we'd always have them as a resource and reference.

Today, modern technology has made life easier and you can avoid *Strong's Concordance* by doing a word search on the Bible App or YouVersion. However, may I suggest that you resist the temptation to copy and paste your findings and stick with writing them down by hand?

I know this seems ridiculous at first glance, but there are actually studies that show that people retain 10 percent of what they *read*, 20 percent of what they *hear*, but 70 percent of what they *say* and *write*.

So take the extra time and invest in writing the Scriptures down yourself. It will help you get more of God's Word into your heart so that it can do its work.

These are just a few of the practical ways that our family applied God's Word to our hearts during our healing process. I believe that, just as it made a radical difference in our lives, it will revolutionize yours.

Of course, it all starts with the same commitment that my friend made when she chose to go to physical therapy so her leg would be healed—the concept is good, but it only works when you keep your commitment.

So before we move on to the next step, here are a few final practicalities that I've found helped me keep my commitment:

1. Block off time in your schedule for Bible study.

Bible study isn't something that can "fit into your schedule." You can't do it on the fly. If understanding the Bible so that you can practically apply it to your life is important to you, then you need to schedule time into your day for dedicated Bible study.

How do you do this? Well, I once read that Franklin Graham's mom would get up before everyone else in her house for the exclusive purpose of Bible study.

Other women choose to set aside time after everyone else has gone to bed, or they designate a free hour during the day when the kids are in school to dedicate time to this pursuit.

My mom always set aside time in the afternoon—after the chores were done in the morning and before we'd get home from school or she needed to prepare dinner.

The important thing isn't exactly *when* you choose to schedule time to study the Bible, but that you *do* schedule time to study the Bible. You know your schedule and what works for you better than anyone else. Just like you'd schedule an appointment to work out or go to the gym to strengthen your physical body, schedule appointments throughout your week to study the Bible to strengthen your spiritual self. Remember: It will only happen if you make it happen.

2. Find a private place to study.

Fact: You're never going to be able to concentrate on your studies if you are constantly being interrupted. So find a quiet place where you can set up your Bible, your resource books, and your computer just as if you were studying a course in school. It would be great if you could find a place where you could leave everything set up from study session to study session (some women actually do this); however, it isn't necessary. If your house is small, like mine, you'll have to clean up in between study sessions, but it can be done. I do it and so can you!

3. Don't be overwhelmed.

I know it can seem like a lot of information to digest and it's easy to become overwhelmed and just say, "It's too hard!" But it really isn't that hard and the benefits are so worth it.

If you're serious about experiencing freedom and healing in your life, there comes a point where we need to stop making excuses, take a cue from Nike, and "Just Do It."

Start somewhere.

> *If you're serious about experiencing freedom and healing in your life, there comes a point where you need to stop making excuses, and "Just Do It."*

Determine that God's Word is important in your life, put it at the top of your priority list, and make time to do it.

It's when you make that decision you'll start reading God's Word, building spiritual muscle, and finding strength for the journey. As you commit to the discipline of Bible study on a regular basis, you'll soon find that you have a greater understanding of the Bible and you'll find more and more ways to practically apply it to your life.

Most importantly, you'll be on the road to health, recovery, and freedom, and you'll begin experiencing the amazing life Jesus has for you.

Chapter 13

Investing in Counseling

There comes a point in all of our lives when we need help.

When we don't know what to do, which way to turn, or how to help ourselves. It's during these times that we need back-up, reinforcements—someone else to offer guidance, advice, and wisdom so that we can see through the fog and get back on the right path again. This is the purpose of counseling—the next tool we're going to discuss as we talk about gaining freedom and healing.

Throughout our lives, our family found Christian counselors to be very helpful. In fact, no more than three months passed after my mom became a Christian when she found herself in the office of a local Christian counseling center.

You see, when she completely surrendered her life to Jesus and allowed the Holy Spirit free rein to heal her of anything in her past, she almost immediately began remembering the trauma of being molested as a child. At first, she had absolutely no idea what was going on—after all, she'd repressed this for years. It wasn't until a woman who was further along on her spiritual journey came and explained that the Holy

Spirit was simply trying to heal her heart so that she could be set free that she understood that inner healing was a normal part of the Christian experience. Her friend then helped her find a Bible-based, Spirit-filled counseling center that not only helped her work through this memory, but also taught her the basic principles of how to go through the process of inner healing on her own.

Many of the principles in this book are things that Mom learned over forty years ago from her counselors. So, from the very beginning, we saw the value of counseling.

I've also found counseling to be very helpful in my own life.

Even before I started my journey to healing and freedom, I remember going to a counselor when we had to change schools, when I was struggling with issues of insecurity and self-esteem in high school, and when my college friend committed suicide.

When I came home from college, heartbroken and devastated, it was a pastoral counselor who didn't coddle me or say "Poor Adessa," but gave me books to read and challenged me to start taking steps toward dealing with the issues in my heart and mind.

Then came the hardest times—when all of the secrets, lies, abuse, and debt were discovered. Individually and as a family, we went through counseling, including working with a pastor who specialized in helping people overcome generational iniquities. Honestly, I don't know what we would have done without this man and his wife who were there for us any time, day or night, to pray with us, give us advice, and just help us see the right way to go.

I'll also always be grateful to a local Assemblies of God pastor who offered us free counseling after Mom went to heaven. At a time in life when I felt like I'd lost everything and had to start all over again, he helped us find our way, establish boundaries with my dad, and get our lives started again.

So beyond a doubt, I am a firm believer that there are times in life when a born-again, Spirit-filled counselor is absolutely necessary.

Here's another thing that I've learned:

One of the biggest tools that the enemy will use to keep you from walking in health and freedom is the lie that counseling isn't needed. Just about the time you're ready to make the phone call and set up an appointment, thoughts will go through your mind like, "Why are you being such a baby? This is not a big deal—you're just being a drama queen. You can handle this on your own, you don't need to go to a counselor and waste the time and money."

Please allow me to be blunt: **These thoughts are just a big bunch of bologna!**

They are lies! The goal is to keep you from getting help, seeing truth, discovering the right path and walking on it.

Don't fall for it!

Instead, when you start thinking this way, follow through and make the call. Keep pursuing freedom.

The truth is that counseling is NOT a waste of time or money.

No, it is an investment in your most important assets—your heart and mind.

When you sacrifice the time and money to really pursue freedom, it's an investment that will pay off for the rest of your life. Not only your life, but also the lives of every generation that comes after you who can then build on your foundation of freedom rather than having to blaze their own trail of overcoming the sins and bondages passed down from generation to generation.

Freedom and healing are ALWAYS worth the investment! So don't believe the lies. Instead, pursue healing with everything that you have. If you need the help of a counselor to see what avenues you should to take to pursue freedom, then find a counselor, and get on the road to healing as soon as possible.

Of course, not all counselors are created equal. Even though most counselors are well trained and have good intentions, if you really want to experience true healing and freedom, it's very important that you find a born-again, Bible-believing, preferably Holy Spirit-filled counselor.

Psalm 1:1 (NKJV) says, **"Blessed is the man who walks not in the counsel of the ungodly, nor stands in the paths of sinners, nor sits in the seat of the scornful; but his delight is in the law of the Lord, and in His law he meditates day and night."**

Because true health and freedom can only be found in the truth of God's Word, it is very important that you find a counselor who will give you advice and wisdom that comes from and agrees with the Word of God.

Recently, I heard a story about a woman who was struggling with issues of insecurity. Wanting to overcome, she went to a counselor that was very well-meaning, but not a Christian. Her counselor encouraged her to step outside of her comfort zone and become sexually active, believing this would help her overcome her inhibitions. Taking her counselor's advice, the woman began living a sinful lifestyle that only resulted in more pain and frustration. It wasn't until a godly friend helped her see that although her counselor meant well, the advice she'd received was totally wrong. Together they found a godly counselor who then had to begin by repairing the damage caused by the ungodly counselor's advice.

Friends, I don't want to see this happen to you. The only way to keep this from happening is to find a counselor who loves Jesus, is committed to living a godly life based on biblical principles, and is teaching those principles to their clients. The truth is that the Bible gives us all of the answers that we need for how to live a healthy, holy, full life in Jesus. A godly counselor will help you find those answers, but a counselor who doesn't know Jesus and believe in the Bible will lead you away from the answers you need and into empty ideas and philosophies.

As important as it is to seek counsel, you need to make sure that it is godly, Bible-based counsel that delights in God's laws. As it says in Psalm 1, that is the way to prosperity. Anything else will keep leading you down the path to pain.

How do you know if a counselor is a godly counselor?

One way is to ask the godly people in your life for recommendations.

Ask your pastor if he or she can recommend someone. Many churches offer counseling as part of their ministry. If your church doesn't, ask your pastor for a recommendation of a trusted church that does. A good pastor will not see this as competition, but rather will understand that the body of Christ works together to help people.

There are also Christian counseling centers available. Again, your pastor or the staff at your church may be able to recommend a center in your area.

Don't just go online and pick anyone. Instead, check them out.

Even if it's a Christian counseling center, read through their statement of beliefs.

Call them and ask for references.

Talk to a godly person that you trust and see if the center is trustworthy and reliable.

I'll be honest and tell you that this is exactly what we did before we started working with the pastor who specialized in helping people overcome generational iniquities. Even though we knew he was a local pastor with a good reputation, we still weren't sure, so we contacted people who knew him and people we trusted. When the man who had been our pastor for years said, *"Yes, I know him, he's trustworthy and reliable, a godly man who will only give you truth from the Bible"*—that's when we made the call and set up an appointment.

I'd advise anyone to do the same.

Be wise when you pick a counselor. Choose someone who will give you godly advice. Then make the call and start getting the help you need.

> *Counseling is not a waste of time or money. It's an investment in your most important asset—your heart and mind.*

Here are two last thoughts about counseling that we've learned from our experiences:

1. Don't expect counseling to be magic.

Here's the deep, dark truth about counseling: **It only works if you do the work required.**

Sorry, but it isn't magical.

Simply going to counseling and getting wise, godly counsel isn't going to change your situation.

Nothing will change until you leave the office and start taking the advice and putting godly principles to work in your life. You see, counseling is only meant to help you find which way to go. At the end of the day, the choice still rests with you as to whether or not you will go there.

One of the reasons that my dad went through counselor after counselor without changing is that he'd leave their office and not do what they told him to do. Nothing changed.

I remember one time in particular when I was in college and commuting with my dad to work for a summer job. While we were waiting for our ride to arrive, he was telling me about the counseling session he'd been in with a very godly counselor the day before. After he told me some of the very practical, very good advice he was given, he ended with the excuses for why it didn't apply to him and that the counselor just didn't understand.

I remember thinking, "What's wrong with you? That was great advice."

Still, because he rejected it, the counseling did nothing to help him. The situation grew worse and worse, until years later the Holy Spirit had to reveal my dad's sins in a very dramatic fashion.

This pattern happened more than once. Honestly, my dad wasted a lot of counselors' time and his money because he didn't want to change. He went to counseling to get people off his back, but rejected everything he was told. Counseling didn't help him at all.

On the other hand, when it came time for my mom, Jamie, and me to go to counseling, we took the exact opposite approach. We did everything the counselors recommended as well as we possibly could because we were starving for healing and freedom.

In the end, that's what determines whether or not counseling will work:

Finding Healing

Do you want change enough to do the work involved in healing?
Will you take the advice you're given?
Will you allow the Holy Spirit to help you remember?
Will you forgive?
Will you make changes?
Are you willing to do whatever it takes to be free?

Counseling is a great tool in the hands of someone who is willing to take advice. It can be life changing. However, it isn't magic. So before you make the appointment **decide in your heart that you're going to do the work necessary and make the changes necessary to overcome. That's when counseling will work for you.**

Here's the deep dark truth about counseling: It only works if you do the work required.

2. Counseling only works when you're honest.

Again, this is something we learned from my dad's experience.

You see, counselors aren't mind readers. They can only work with the information you give them. Even the most Spirit-filled counselors with the gift of discernment can only help you if you are honest with them and honest with yourself.

That's another reason that counseling didn't work for my dad. He'd essentially go into a counselor's office and lie. He'd put on an act or a show that he was one way and then come home and be completely different.

In fact, it got so bad that my mom had to stop going to marriage counseling with him because he'd go to the counselor's office, play the role of the remorseful cooperative husband who wanted to do whatever was necessary to save the marriage, and the counselors would applaud his attitude and start placing the blame on my mom. After the counseling session, feeling empowered by the counselor's applause, my dad would then get in the car and start abusing my mom. It was a horrible cycle based on a lie. Counseling never worked because real problems were never brought to the table and addressed so that a solution could be found.

This didn't just happen in marriage counseling. Because my dad was lying about all parts of his life, his counselors never really got to know him. The few who did see through the charade and start challenging his lies were written off as "crazy" and he moved on. He went through counselor after counselor with no help because he wouldn't tell the truth.

It wasn't until the secrets were discovered and the lies revealed that we (Mom, Jamie, and I) could go to a counselor, tell the truth, and really get help. When they were given the truth, they could help us formulate a Bible-based plan to help us heal and overcome each issue and situation.

You see, going to a counselor's office and lying is like going to a doctor's office and asking them to guess how to treat you as you lie about your symptoms and medical history. Actually, it is easier for a physical doctor to figure out because they can run tests. A counselor doesn't have a scientific way to decipher truth from lies.

As someone who has gone through the experience over and over again of watching a counselor try to find truth among the lies, please let me encourage you that when you go to a counselor, tell them the truth the whole truth and nothing but the truth.

Don't try to make yourself look good, manipulate the outcome, or withhold information. These choices won't help you at all.

Instead, when you go to a counselor, be real, be open, be honest, and be vulnerable. Lay it all on the table so that you can get the help and advice that you need so that you can start healing.

Because that's the goal: healing and freedom.

If you go into a Christian, Bible-believing counselor's office with an honest, open heart, prepared to receive wise counsel and obey it, it will be a life-changing investment. Their years of study and wisdom can help you know exactly what steps you need to take to gain health and freedom.

I know because it happened in my life. That's why I encourage you to find a godly counselor. Be honest. Be open. Go in prepared to work and then go after your healing with all you've got! Invest in yourself and experience all Jesus has for you!

> When you go to a counselor, tell them the truth, the whole truth, and nothing but the truth.

Chapter 14

Forgiveness

The next step I found to be a key ingredient on the road to healing is a topic that just sends terror into the hearts of many women. That is the topic of forgiveness.

I'll be honest and admit that for many years I would hear someone say they were going to talk about forgiveness and my back would tighten up and I would get knots in my stomach because I knew it was going to be some kind of a guilt trip telling me that I had to let someone's bad behavior go without explanation or repentance. Other times I'd feel like there was something wrong with me that I was still struggling with pain from being hurt.

Why?

Well, it wasn't that I didn't believe it is important. Quite the opposite.

The Bible is clear that forgiveness is a key principle in God's kingdom. Jesus said in Mark 11:25, **"And when you stand praying, if you hold anything against anyone, forgive them, so that your Father in heaven may forgive you your sins."**

God ties our willingness to forgive others with his willingness to forgive us. I don't know about you, but I don't want anything standing between my sins and God's forgiveness. And even though I try not to, I still do more than enough things wrong to know that I need to be forgiven—daily.

Wanting to be forgiven by God isn't the only reason I believe in forgiveness. Personally, I have seen and experienced the healing power of forgiveness in my own life. I've been on the receiving end of people who have extended grace, forgiveness, and a second chance in my direction even when I didn't deserve it. I've also seen God work miracles in my heart that have allowed me the strength, courage, and emotional healing to extend grace to people who didn't deserve it.

Of course, we grew up with Mom teaching us that forgiveness was an important key to healing all of the wounds in your heart. From a very early age, we saw her implementing the steps of forgiveness she learned in counseling, in a very practical way.

Jamie and I were there in the background when she'd go and talk to relatives, asking them to forgive her and telling them she forgave them for things done in the past. We watched as she put these principles into practice after she was very hurt during a traumatic church split when we were very young. Time and again I saw her forgive my dad throughout their marriage. Through her example, we didn't just hear about forgiveness, but we saw the power of it in action.

Even in my own life, I had experienced the power of working through the steps of forgiveness. I remember as a teenager there was a young man in youth group who would boost his self-esteem by picking on the weaker links in the group. Being new to the group, that was me. Although I understand his motivation now, at the time all I could feel was the pain of his words that left me feeling humiliated.

Even though my first response was to be angry, hate him, and even want to retaliate, I knew from my mom's teaching and Bible study that this was wrong. So instead, I chose to follow the steps and pray about the matter, daily pray blessings on him, try to do good things for him, and try to see God's purpose in his life. Much to my surprise, these steps worked! In time my heart changed, and I was actually able to pray for him and encourage him when he went through a very difficult time.

So going into my time of healing, I was a true believer in the power of forgiveness.

Still, when it came to the topic of forgiving my dad for all the hurt and pain he'd caused me, my mom, and my brother, and all the damage he did to our lives, it seemed almost impossible.

The main reason that I think I struggled and that many other people struggle with forgiveness is that I didn't really understand it. A lot of my misunderstandings of forgiveness were tying me up in knots. I mean, up until this point the offenses I'd had to forgive were much less traumatic and damaging. Or they involved people who weren't involved in our everyday lives—it was more situational than all-encompassing.

When it came to forgiving my dad, I struggled with questions like:

What do I do with all the emotional pain that I still feel?

Why can't I just forget and pretend that things are all "hunky dory"?

How can I fix a relationship with someone who is content with the current relationship?

How do I forgive someone who isn't sorry and doesn't want to change?

Then of course, I'd feel guilty because I knew that God wanted me to forgive. Over and over again this roller-coaster ride continued.

Until I began to understand what forgiveness was and what it was not.

This changed my life!

First of all, **forgiveness is not condoning the other person's behavior as acceptable or no big deal.**

You see, one of the reasons that forgiveness was so hard for me is that I saw forgiveness as a get-out-of-jail-free card for people who weren't really sorry and didn't want to change their lives. The truth is that you don't want to tell the person who hurt you and changed your life that everything they did is all right.

One thing that helped me was when the Holy Spirit showed me that to forgive you have to acknowledge that the other person hurt you and damaged you. You admit that they were wrong. An offense occurred—what they did wasn't all right—that's why you need to forgive them.

> *To forgive you have to acknowledge that the other person hurt you and damaged you. An offense occurred—what they did wasn't all right—that's why you need to forgive them.*

When I realized that forgiveness wasn't saying, "Oh, it's okay that you did this or it's no big deal," that's when I could put things into perspective and stop blaming myself for the pain inside my heart.

Forgiveness doesn't mean you have to forget.

Realistically, you can't forget what happened. It's part of your story. I mean, how could I "forget" decades of my life? You can't.

What forgiveness will do is heal your heart and take away the pain when you remember. That's how I can write this book or tell my story in a sermon: because it doesn't hurt anymore. I can't forget the facts, but I no longer have to live trapped in the pain.

Forgiveness doesn't mean you don't bring it up again.

Talking about issues is the key to freedom. Talking is healthy. Suppressing hurts and keeping secrets is unhealthy. God wants us to be healthy.

Forgiveness doesn't mean you have to put your heart on the line to be hurt by someone who is unrepentant and unchanged.

Just because God commands us to forgive does not mean that he wants us to allow people to abuse us, demean us, or diminish our dignity without establishing boundaries.

That would be unwise. God wants his children to be wise. Healthy boundaries are choices that you make to proceed in a safer, healthier, more beneficial manner with the goal of living a peaceful life.

Once the Holy Spirit removed my fear of forgiveness by showing me what forgiveness was not, then I was able to understand what forgiveness is and start to experience its healing power in my life.

Over the years what I've come to learn is that forgiveness is not about the other person. Forgiveness is a gift you give yourself.

So what is forgiveness?

Forgiveness is a choice that we make to follow God and choose to forgive someone who hurt us.

Forgiveness is the ointment that keeps you from being tied up in knots of hate, anger, and resentment.

As long as you don't forgive them, they are still hurting you and controlling your life. You are still the other person's prisoner. When you can say, "I know you were wrong, but I forgive you," you are releasing yourself from all the power the other person has over you. That opens the door for God's healing power to do a miracle in your heart.

Forgiveness is about setting yourself free to experience God's love and healing regardless of what happens to the other person.

Think of it like this: The person who hurt you took a can of paint and threw it at you for no good reason. They made a cruel decision or decisions and they were wrong.

However, you are the one covered in paint. Unless you wash the paint off of your skin and your clothes, that paint isn't going to go away.

Forgiveness is the first step in washing the paint from your skin.

Forgiveness is saying **"I'm not going to let your choices affect the rest of my life. I am going to do whatever is necessary to pursue healing and freedom."**

Forgiveness is a crucial step in healing. It is impossible to heal without it. Even though it isn't always easy, your personal journey to healing and freedom cannot start until you make the decision that you are going to forgive.

How do you do it?

The only way I know to answer this question is to tell you what we did and how it helped us. Jamie and I were so

Chapter 14 — Forgiveness

blessed to have our mom with us through most of our journey to healing and freedom. She served as our mentor and taught us many things she'd learned on her own spiritual journey. When we came to the point where we were faced with the question of having to daily forgive Dad for how he was hurting her, hurting us, and causing so much pain in our family, it was hard. Remember, we were working through forgiving him for things he'd done in the past as well as living with his bad choices every day. Honestly, there were days when forgiveness seemed impossible.

Then my mom told us a few ways she had learned to help change her heart to forgive. These were the principles we applied to our lives and they helped. I now want to share them with you.

First, understand that forgiveness is not a feeling, it's a choice.

It doesn't matter if you feel you can't forgive someone. You can't wait for this feeling to come. Forgiveness is not an emotion. It is a mental decision you need to make. You must consciously decide, "I am going to forgive that person." It has to be a decision you make of your own free will.

> *Forgiveness is the ointment that keeps you from being tied up in knots of hate, anger, and resentment.*

When God first started dealing with me about the need to forgive, he showed me that I had to do it even if I didn't feel like it. I had to daily decide to forgive my dad.

Sometimes it mean saying over and over again—sometimes twenty times a day choosing again and again—"I am going to forgive him," even when I didn't want to.

Finding Healing

But that's the point—it isn't about the "want to"—it's a matter of obedience. We forgive because we are forgiven and God commands it.

Don't worry about feeling it—the feeling of forgiveness may take time to come. Just keep choosing to forgive because you want to be free.

If we want to experience freedom and healing we need to choose to forgive.

Next, we need to confess our sin of unforgiveness to God.

I know, it sounds crazy. We get hurt and then we have to ask God to forgive us for how we feel?

Yep.

Here's why we do it—-the root of almost all anger, hate, and rage is unforgiveness.

If we allow the sin of unforgiveness to take root in our hearts—no matter how justified it may be—these sins and more will grow from that root and blossom in our lives. We ask God to forgive us for all of the sinful attitudes, thoughts, words, and actions that are in our hearts and lives from our pain, so that we can nip any sin that wants to grow from the unforgiveness at the root.

> *Forgiveness is about setting yourself free to experience God's love and healing regardless of what happens to the other person.*

As we keep short accounts with God and keep our souls clean, the Holy Spirit is free to do a healing work in our hearts.

Next, ask God to bless the person that you need to forgive.

Chapter 14 ~ Forgiveness

Again, I get this is hard—especially when everything inside of you doesn't want them to be blessed but instead wants them to pay.

Praying for someone who needs to be forgiven is like putting healing ointment on your own wound. As you pray, God is using your prayer to not only change that person, but he's using it to heal your heart.

Jesus commanded us to bless those who spitefully use us. We need to follow this pattern. Ask God to bless the person, provide for their needs, and to help them become all that he wants them to be.

I believe that one of the reasons God commands us to do this is because in time, it is hard to feel hate and unforgiveness while praying for the person's good.

Here's another tip: **Do something nice for the person.**

Luke 6:27–36 says: **"But to you who are listening I say: Love your enemies, do good to those who hate you, bless those who curse you, pray for those who mistreat you. If someone slaps you on one cheek, turn to them the other also. If someone takes your coat, do not withhold your shirt from them. Give to everyone who asks you, and if anyone takes what belongs to you, do not demand it back. Do to others as you would have them do to you.**

"If you love those who love you, what credit is that to you? Even sinners love those who love them. And if you do good to those who are good to you, what credit is that to you? Even sinners do that. And if you lend to those from whom you expect repayment, what credit is that to you? Even sinners lend to sinners, expecting to be repaid in full. But love your enemies, do good to

Finding Healing

them, and lend to them without expecting to get anything back. Then your reward will be great, and you will be children of the Most High, because he is kind to the ungrateful and wicked. Be merciful, just as your Father is merciful."

I'm going to be very honest and say that this was not easy for me or my brother—especially after my mom went to heaven.

The truth is that after she died, we were done. Our goal was to get away from my dad and never look back. Maybe a Christmas card—maybe not.

We were just done. We'd had enough of the pain, the abuse, and his unwillingness to change. There were days when even just looking at him or having to talk to him as we were grieving and remembering the horrific way he treated Mom were almost impossible.

Our plan was as soon as possible, we were out the door.

Only God had another plan.

It wasn't long until the Holy Spirit spoke to our hearts and said, "No, you're not leaving. You are going to stay and show my love to your dad."

Are you kidding me?

How could God expect this?

Yet, it was as we obeyed and continued showing love to my dad—

> *If we allow the sin of unforgiveness to take root in our hearts—no matter how justified it may be—these sins and more will grow from that root and blossom in our lives.*

Chapter 14 — Forgiveness

cooking for him, cleaning the house, taking care of his finances, and just simply not abandoning him—that we healed.

I believe this choice is the reason that my dad chose to go back to church and give Christianity another try. I truly believe if we would have left, he'd have chosen another direction.

Even more, it was out of this choice to forgive that our testimony was formed. I mean, how could we honestly say that God is able to heal and set people free through forgiveness if we were not willing to forgive?

Yet, today I can say that if you forgive even when it's hard—even when the offense seems unforgiveable—God can heal your heart. Today, I am no longer walking around hurting, bitter, and broken, but I am strong, healthy, and able to function not out of a place of emotion, but from a rational perspective where I make intelligent choices and do the right thing.

Not only will he heal your heart, but he'll work miraculously through your choice to touch the lives of other people.

Please don't think this was a once and done choice. Far from it!

The choice to forgive my dad, to talk to him kindly, to do things for him, and treat him as Jesus would was a choice we had to make almost daily at first. It wasn't easy. Yet, it was what we needed to do.

For probably the first three years after Mom went to heaven, God and I would discuss "Can we leave now?" This was usually followed by a "But you don't understand!"

Yet, nobody understands forgiveness better than Jesus.

If ever there was a man who had the right to harbor unforgiveness, it was Jesus. He was beaten, almost to death. He was mocked. He was spit upon. He was ridiculed, despised, and abused. He was hung on a cross even though he was totally innocent and sinless. He had every reason in the word to hate, be angry, and seek vengeance. He had every right in the world to destroy everyone around the cross for what they did to him, and he had the power and ability to do it.

But he didn't! Instead, he asked his Father to forgive them! He did good to his enemies. We need to do the same.

In the same spirit we need to remember that:

Forgiveness also means that we give up the right to retaliate.

Instead, we trust God to be our avenger and fight our battles for us. This is difficult because when we hurt, we want the person who hurt us to hurt. When we choose to follow Christ, we need to choose a different path and let God deal with the person who hurt us. Meanwhile, we need to try to treat that person with respect and dignity. If we are trying to do this, we are on the road of forgiveness.

Here's one final thing that my mom taught us about forgiveness:

While forgiveness is absolutely necessary, you can't condone their evil behavior.

Forgiveness doesn't mean you allow the person to keep sinning against you.

> *Praying for someone who needs to be forgiven is like putting healing ointment on your own wound. As you pray, God is using your prayer to not only change that person, but he's using it to heal your heart.*

Chapter 14 — Forgiveness

Today as I write this chapter I can say in good conscience that through the power of the Holy Spirit, I have forgiven my dad. However, my forgiveness is not a license for him to be abusive.

Although most of the dramatic outbursts and violent situations have stopped since he went back to church, there are still times when his manipulative, controlling tactics of emotional abuse try to resurface. When this happens, I lovingly confront him and let him know it is unacceptable and WILL NOT continue. However, I don't allow hatred, anger, or unforgiveness to take root inside of me either.

For instance, recently my dad had an outburst. He meant to scare and intimidate us in order to get his own way.

But because of the healing power of Jesus in our lives, it didn't work out.

Instead of becoming afraid, losing our tempers, or allowing anger, rage, or unforgiveness to consume us, I told him this behavior was unacceptable and he had to stop and get control of himself. Then I went on with the rest of the day.

True forgiveness allows you to take a stand against the evil behavior while not allowing anger, bitterness, and hate to consume you. That's the goal: your freedom and healing!

Basically, these are the steps to forgiveness that helped my mom, my brother and me experience forgiveness, freedom, and healing in our own lives. Over the years, they haven't just helped us deal with the pain we had toward my dad, but toward almost anyone who has caused us pain.

Today, I don't know what pain you're facing in your heart.

It may be more or less dramatic than mine, and you may feel like you have more or less to forgive. In the end, what matters is that for each of us, forgiveness is a necessary ingredient to gaining freedom, joy, and healing. There's no detour around it. Forgiveness is the only road.

Healing for your heart, your soul, and your mind is available when you apply the principles of the Bible like ointment to your life. As you choose to live by God's Word, you will become stronger, healthier, and more able to overcome the obstacles of life rather than be defeated by them.

As you obtain victory, you're gaining more and more ground on the road to healing and freedom.

Chapter 15

Forgiving God

In the last chapter, we talked about the importance of forgiving those who hurt us so that we can be healed.

In this chapter, we're going to take the topic of forgiveness a step further and talk about the need to forgive God. (I know, it almost sounds sacrilegious and, dare I even say, sinful.)

Yet, one of the choices that you need to make on your journey to living a joyful, fulfilled, victorious life is openly and honestly dealing with God. It's time to lay your cards on the table.

Your life didn't turn out the way you hoped or planned.

God is supposed to be in control of your life and whether you're allowing yourself to openly ask this question or not, there's a place in your heart that's saying, "How could God let this happen to me?"

No matter how many times you read an inspirational Scripture or listened to a "Buck up Baby, everything is going to be all right" praise and worship song, deep inside your heart YOU ARE ANGRY.

I can tell you from experience that until you deal with your anger toward God, you will not be able to make any of the other choices that will lead to a happy and fulfilled life.

This was absolutely something I had to face on my journey to healing.

Because let's be honest—the detour that God planned for my life was never on my "to do" list. Even though I loved Jesus and had completely surrendered my life to him, the reality was that there were days when I was ANGRY. Every ounce of emotion was being pointed directly at God saying, "This is YOUR fault!"

I had two choices: I could allow my anger and disappointment to continue controlling me, abandon my commitment to follow God's plan for my life, take the reins and start pursuing my own dreams, or I could get real with God, face my anger, pain, and disappointment, reconcile our relationship, and get back to the business of following Jesus via the on-ramp of surrender.

Heart to heart, sister to sister, from a heart of love I need to tell you that each of us needs to come to the place where we choose between these two options.

Are you going to deal with your anger or let it control you?

Will you even admit it's there or will you keep denying it and running away from it?

Are you ready to get real with God or will you keep walking away from him?

I know it seems like there should be a third option. It sounds harsh to say that you can't continue to harbor anger and resentment toward God in your heart and follow him. But it's true.

Chapter 15 ~ Forgiving God

You see, God wants to have an intimate and personal relationship with you. When you don't deal with your anger and pain it becomes a barrier in that relationship, causing you and God to grow further and further apart. Even though you may still call yourself a Christian, be involved in church, and do all the right things, until you actually take down the wall of anger and pain, it will always stand in the way of developing a healthy relationship with God.

It's like the married couple who still lives in the same house, still files joint tax returns and still shows up together at parties, but inside the house they don't talk, they live separate lives, and even sleep in separate rooms. It looks like they are married, but they don't really have a married relationship. He lives his life and she lives hers. It's a charade.

There are lots of Christians who are living the same charade with God. Technically, they are going through all the motions of being a Christian, but the truth is that at some point they let anger, heartache, or disappointments destroy their relationship with him. Rather than facing the fact that they had issues with God, they chose to let those issues become a giant wall. Because of unresolved issues, they live their lives the way they want to and check in with God when it's appropriate. Some walk away from God altogether, but many more simply fall into the pattern of a loveless, fruitless version of Christianity.

They have a relationship with their pain and anger, but not with God.

Sadly, I've known too many people who make this choice. When faced with genuine disappointment, heartache, or tragedy, they did not choose to get real with God. Without actually saying the words, their actions said, "God let too many bad things happen to me, he let me suffer too much pain—

Finding Healing

I'm done trusting him. I'll handle things from now on. I'll keep going to church and saying I'm a Christian—but I'm in control now." Either consciously or unconsciously, they make the choice to let unforgiveness toward God rule their lives.

My prayer for you as you're reading this chapter is that you will not repeat their tragic decision. No matter what circumstances caused the anger and pain in your life today, whether it be the death of someone you loved, a divorce, a life-altering disappointment, an unexpected disease, or any other painful situation, I hope that this chapter will help you to choose a different road. Rather than allowing your feelings and pain to destroy your relationship with God, make the choice to do whatever is necessary to restore your relationship with him.

> You can't continue to harbor anger and resentment toward God in your heart and follow him.

Understand that it's okay to be honest with God.

He is not shocked at all by the way that you feel. There is nothing that you could tell him that would surprise him, offend him, or make him stop loving you.

He already knows what's going on inside of you. He sees every tear that you cry and he hears every angry thought and accusation that passes through your mind. He is already aware that you're angry with him. In his compassion he sees beyond the anger into the confusion and pain and fear at the heart of it all.

He's not waiting to judge you or condemn you for these emotions. Instead, he's calling to you saying, **"Come, let us reason together.**

Chapter 15 ~ Forgiving God

"Let's deal with this—let's talk it out. Together we'll get it all out in the open, deal with the pain in your heart, begin the healing process, and move forward together."

That's our heavenly Father's heart.

Healing. Restoration. Renewed fellowship. This is what he desires.

It all begins when you make the choice to get real with God.

At this point, some of you may be asking, **"But how do I begin?"**

Perhaps the idea of being completely open and honest with God is a new concept for you and you're wondering, *"Is it really okay to be totally vulnerable with God? After all, he is God."*

Let me assure you that I've learned from personal experience that the best place to start is with total, complete, and open honesty. Get alone with God and tell him exactly how you feel.

Please, trust me when I say that it's nothing he hasn't already heard before.

Don't believe me? Take a quick perusal through the Psalms and the Prophetic Books. These books of the Bible are filled with godly people who had deep, intimate relationships with God, pouring out their hearts and sharing the good, the bad, and the "oh-my-goodness-I-can't-believe-they-just-said-that."

One of my favorite examples is the Old Testament prophet Jeremiah. (The books of Jeremiah and Job also happen to be my two favorite books in the Bible, so read into that what you want.)

Jeremiah was God's man—his mouthpiece to the nation of Israel at this time. Jeremiah was also a really emotional guy. When he had a feeling, he REALLY felt it.

Finding Healing

Throughout the book of Jeremiah, it's obvious that the prophet had some very strong feelings about some of the things God was allowing in his life at the time. Here's a few select passages that will show you what I mean:

Jeremiah 20:7–8 (MSG),

> **You pushed me into this, God, and I let you do it.**
>> **You were too much for me.**
>> **And now I'm a public joke.**
>> **They all poke fun at me.**
>> **Every time I open my mouth**
>> **I'm shouting, "Murder!" or "Rape!"**
>> **And all I get for my God-warnings**
>> **are insults and contempt.**

Look at this one: Jeremiah 15:15–18 (MSG)

> **You know where I am, God! Remember what I'm doing here!**
>> **Take my side against my detractors.**
>> **Don't stand back while they ruin me.**
>> **Just look at the abuse I'm taking!**
>> **When your words showed up, I ate them—**
>> **swallowed them whole. What a feast!**
>> **What delight I took in being yours,**
>> **O God, God-of-the-Angel-Armies!**
>> **I never joined the party crowd**
>> **in their laughter and their fun.**
>> **Led by you, I went off by myself.**
>> **You'd filled me with indignation. Their sin had me seething.**
>> **But why, why this chronic pain,**
>> **this ever worsening wound and no healing in sight?**
>> **You're nothing, God, but a mirage,**
>> **a lovely oasis in the distance—and then nothing!**

Chapter 15 ~ Forgiving God

And you think God is going to be shocked or offended by what's on your heart!

Go through the Bible and see that it is completely normal (even healthy) for God's people to speak to God openly and honestly about their pain, disappointments, and anger toward him. You can see it in the life of Job, David, Moses, Habakkuk, and many other godly men and women who made the choice to get real with God rather than let their anger take root and ruin their relationship with him.

There is nothing wrong with pouring out your heart to God as long as you don't stop there. This is just step one on the road to healing and restoration. As with any relationship, it's perfectly normal for there to be times when the two parties in a relationship sit down and say, *"We've got to talk about some problems and truthfully lay all of the issues on the table."*

There's an old saying that says, "Nothing clears the air like a good fight."

However, after the air is cleared, reconciliation comes when the two opposing sides come together to start picking up the pieces.

It's the same way in your relationship with God: after you've poured out your heart and emptied out your anger, you need to keep moving forward in the process and begin to reconcile your relationship with him.

The next step in reconciliation is your choice to forgive God.

I know it sounds ridiculous and again, maybe even a little like heresy. After all, did God do something wrong that we need to forgive him?

No, God never does anything wrong. He never sins and he never makes a mistake.

Our choice to forgive God has nothing to do with him; it's about us. We need to make the conscious choice to stop blaming God for the things he allowed in our lives.

It's coming to the place of resolving that even though you don't understand why God allowed what he did and you may not even like what he did, you're not going to allow your confusion and pain to build a wall of anger, confusion, and disappointment in your relationship with God. It's basically coming to a place of acceptance where you say, "I don't understand, but I'm going to trust you anyway and put my anger aside."

It is normal and healthy for God's people to speak to God openly and honestly about their pain, disappointments, and anger toward him.

Of course, the next step in reconciling your relationship with God is asking him to forgive you for being angry with him and blaming him.

What?? Didn't you just say it was normal and even healthy to express your anger to God?

Absolutely.

Then why do I have to ask God to forgive me for feeling this way?

Well, just because you honestly feel something doesn't mean that your feelings were right. Being open and honest before God allows us to purge all of the anger, disappointment, feelings of betrayal, and pain from our hearts. Purging is the healthy part.

We ask God to forgive us because even though these feelings may be natural and normal, it is still a sin for us to be angry with God. True restoration of fellowship only comes when we not only admit that the sin is there, but we ask God to forgive it and take it away. That's when the healing process can really begin.

You see, it's not a sin to feel anger toward God in the heat of the moment; however, it is a sin to allow unconfessed anger to take up residence in your heart. When we confess our sin of anger, we're giving it an eviction notice that says, "You're not welcome here anymore . . . I'm choosing my relationship with God over my feelings."

As we talked about at the beginning of the chapter, it's the choice to forgive God and stop blaming him for our lives and to ask his forgiveness for being angry and disappointed in him that puts us back on the on-ramp once again of choosing to surrender our will to God's will and choosing to live contentedly in the circumstances he's allowed.

It's those three steps: Honesty, forgiveness, and surrender that help you get off of the destructive road of anger and take those first few steps toward living in victory and healing.

I know from experience that these choices are not always easy. I'll even warn you that there will be times when those old voices of anger and *"God doesn't really love you or he wouldn't allow these things to happen to you"* may try to reappear.

I know that in my own life, there were years where the struggle between what I wanted and what God wanted would

> *Honesty, forgiveness, and surrender help you get off of the destructive road of anger and take steps toward living in victory and healing.*

try to reemerge, attempting to build a wall in my relationship with God.

Yet, every time, it was my CHOICE to get real with God, say, *"This is how I feel, but I'm setting my feelings aside for the sake of our relationship,"* that helped me stay on God's path for my life and ultimately find satisfaction, peace, and joy.

What I've learned after years of fighting the battle between what I want and what God wants is that even when I can't see it, even when it makes no sense to me, and even when it's painful, God always has a plan to use everything he allows in my life for his good and the good of his kingdom. God doesn't waste anything.

Just like he did in the life of Joseph, a young man who was sold into slavery and then falsely imprisoned because of other people's sinful choices, God can make something good out of every disappointment that has happened in your life. The only thing that can stop God from making a treasure from your tragedy is your choice to let unresolved anger, resentment, or disappointments lead you on a path of rebellion away from God's plan for your life.

Don't make that choice. Instead, every time you want to blame God or be angry with him, make the choice to get real with him.

Be open, be honest, be real, and then be repentant.

Always make the decision to trade your heartache for his healing by bringing your pain to him and re-surrendering your will to his ways. Choose to get real with God and see if you don't ultimately discover that God has a plan and a purpose for every detail in your life.

This choice will help you make big strides on your road to healing.

Chapter 16

Talking and Journaling

*D*id you ever eat something that made you sick?

Perhaps at first you thought it was good, but hours later as you're suffering in pain, you just wish you could expel this nasty poison out of your body.

At the risk of crossing the line into territory that's less than delicate, have you ever felt much better after the food that was making you sick exited your system, even if it was a little traumatic while it was leaving?

I think if we were honest, we've all been there. It's a pretty common human dilemma.

It's also a pretty common issue when we look beyond the physical and begin looking at how to overcome the toxic issues that are filling our hearts and minds with pain. Sometimes you just have to get it out!!

Two of the best ways that I've learned to expel toxins from my heart and mind are **talking** and **journaling**.

These were two things that really helped me and our family tremendously on our road to spiritual healing.

Start with talking.

I am a big believer that we need to get things out in the open. We need to talk about the things that are bothering us so that they aren't always keeping us bound up inside.

One of the biggest things causing our family pain and all kinds of problems was secrets.

Things that we didn't talk about.

You don't bring up *that* topic—you can't address *that* issue.

The only thing that this type of rule and attitude does is keep everybody bound up in knots. You can never actually be healed because the wound can never be fully exposed, addressed, and get the attention that it needs.

That's why I strongly believe that it's important for us to find someone who will listen to us. Someone who will let us talk through our issues and bring everything out into the open.

Now I'll caution you: You can't tell everything to everybody.

We know there are some people who are not trustworthy and they will use what we tell them to hurt us. However, we can't let a few bad apples ruin the whole bunch.

Instead, it's important that you find a woman or several women that you can trust. Maybe talk to your pastor or a pastor's wife or a godly woman that you can trust and you can open your heart up to about what's going on in your life.

Chapter 16 — Talking and Journaling

Don't let the fear of gossips keep you from finding the truly godly people who would be willing to listen and help you through your issues.

When we were finally able to break through the secrets and start openly talking about what was going on in our lives, that was a major step in moving toward into a life of freedom and healing.

I know this isn't always easy. As I said in a previous chapter, there were times and topics when it was hard even to speak words out loud in prayer because of the pain in my heart. Yet, forcing myself to do that, even through the tears, made great strides in setting myself free.

I was also blessed because I could talk openly to my family, especially my mom and brother, about what was going on. Not everyone has that opportunity, but it is important that even if you can't talk to those who are involved in the situation, you find someone—a counselor, a pastor, another godly friend—to talk with and share the issues in your heart.

As you heal, you'll find that it is easier and easier to share your story. Honestly, coming from a background where we didn't talk about our secrets, it was unimaginable years ago that I would ever write a book like this or share our testimony from a stage. Yet, as the Holy Spirit continued to heal our hearts, I found that the more I talked and shared, the less it hurt. Now when I tell people our story I really feel no pain because there is power in talking to set you free.

Yet before I could get to this place, I needed to be told that it was okay to talk about our story. This was a revelation that I received at one of the strangest places—a men's conference.

You see, many times when my brother goes to a men's event, I attend to help him work his table. Very early in our ministry, we went to a men's event in New York that was in

Finding Healing

the very heart of a city. Being a small town girl who hadn't travelled much until that point, I was a little afraid of the area and stayed very close to Jamie.

When he went into the service that night, I tagged along and sat in the back. Even though I technically wasn't supposed to be there, the Holy Spirit used that night to completely change my life as I listened to the men's leader share the testimony of his family from the stage.

I have to say that I was shocked as this leader, who could have stood there and maintained the image that he was great and should have been looked up to, shared the ugliest, darkest failures of his life. He ended by saying, "I'm sharing this so that you can learn from my failures and have a better life."

In that moment, the Holy Spirit lanced my heart and I realized that it is God's will for us to tell our stories. He doesn't want us to stay bound in secrets and shame, but he wants to change us, set us free, and use our stories to be a testimony of his grace and power to redeem in a world that's filled with pain.

From that day forward, I learned the value of talking—not just to God, to my family, or to counselors, but to people who needed to hear our testimony. And the more we talked, the more we healed.

Now I understand that not everyone is in the position to do this. Only you can determine how much is safe and legal to share in your situation. Maybe you'll never share your story from a stage, but as the Holy Spirit gives you opportunity, you can share your story with your children, with trusted friends, or with other women that you know who are in the same situation you've been set free from.

I can promise you that as you talk, you will be healed.

Talking sets people free. It removes the poison from your soul and helps you heal.

Begin journaling.

Another thing that helped me tremendously on my own personal road to healing was the concept of journaling.

I am a huge proponent of journaling! It made a major difference in my life.

Please excuse me if you think this is crude, but I believe that journaling is a lot like the cure for bad food because journaling allows you to take all of the toxins and poisons that are making your heart and mind sick and just get them out of your system. You're almost puking it out onto a piece of paper.

The great thing about journaling is that you can say ANYTHING.

You can write down how much you hate a person or situation, how horrible you think they are, how wrong they treated you, how you wish bad things would happen to them while you watched—you can say whatever!

You can get every single bad emotion that you have out of you.

And then you destroy it. Burn it or shred it because you don't need to keep it around.

Still, it's out of you. It's not acting like a poison in your heart and mind anymore. It's not harming you anymore. And because you wrote it down instead of spoke it, you didn't spew all of your feelings at someone and spread them.

Yet, it's all out from inside of you.

I cannot tell you how many journals I filled with genuine feelings that I needed to release from my heart and mind

Finding Healing

so that I could be honest with myself, be honest with God, repent of my feelings, move on and go forward in health.

Because these two methods worked so well for me, I believe they will work for you.

So talk, talk, talk and journal, journal, journal—-it will help you get on the road to healing and freedom.

Chapter 17

Lifestyle Changes

It happens in doctor's offices all over the country. While it's certainly not the most dreaded diagnosis, it may be the most challenging.

"You need to make lifestyle changes."

Although we're grateful to hear that we don't need medicine or a surgery, it's still hard to hear:

You need to change your diet.

You need to exercise.

Reduce stress at work.

Avoid allergens.

It's time to change. As we all know, change is difficult.

As we've said throughout this section, often times the principles of healing in our physical bodies mirror what's necessary to gain spiritual and emotional healing. This is especially true when it comes to the topic of lifestyle changes or behavior modification. The reality is that no matter how much you pray, read the Bible, or visit a counselor, in the end, whether or not your heart is healed and you obtain the abundant life Jesus has for you depends on how seriously you obey the Holy Spirit's diagnosis for behavior modification.

I know this was certainly true in our lives.

For instance, I mentioned before that when my dad's lies were being uncovered, the Holy Spirit used this time to point out that root of lying was slowly infiltrating its way into my life. Although until that point, I'd basically ignored it as a "sinlet," seeing it as no big deal, the Holy Spirit began showing me that it's the little foxes that spoil the grapes (Song of Solomon 2:15) and I needed to deal with this generational iniquity before it grew out of proportion and destroyed my life.

In addition to repenting of this sin and making lists of every time I'd lied, the Holy Spirit required me to discipline myself to speak only truth all of the time. If what I said wasn't 100 percent truthful, then I had to correct it. This wasn't as easy as it sounds. It took a lot of work and there were many times when I had to go back and correct myself.

I remember one bad habit I'd picked up was rounding down whenever I said how much I paid for something. For instance if I paid $9.99 I'd say I paid $9 to make it look like I spent less. While going through this process the Holy Spirit taught me to say $9.99 or $10 (which was closer to the truth).

What's the big deal?

Well, it wasn't about the 99 cents. It was about speaking truth and overcoming the stronghold of lying to make things seem better. It was a "behavior modification" that I had to make so that I could completely overcome and conquer this sin that had caused so much destruction in my family.

Another big area where I had to modify my behavior came in the category of entertainment. You see, I've always been a big fan of romantic music and dramatic stories. Even though I was raised better, when I went to college I indulged myself in romantic, secular music, chick flicks and television shows that I should not have been watching. I was like a

Chapter 17 — Lifestyle Changes

person who gorged herself on unhealthy food and then wondered why she felt sick afterward.

After four years of entertainment choices that did nothing but feed my already twisted thinking about love, sensuality, relationships, and what made a woman attractive, it was time to end their influence. I went cold turkey and began starving some avenues that were creating appetites in my life that were contrary to God's plan and God's will. Specifically, I stopped listening to all secular music, and dramatically edited the quality of my TV and movie choices. I also gave up all fiction material, stopped reading all non-Christian woman's magazines or any other written material that was influencing my thought process.

In a way, I was going through a spiritual cleansing—purging my heart and mind of every influence that wasn't benefiting me. Let me tell you, it wasn't easy. But it was so beneficial.

You see, it wasn't until I repented of focusing on things that were impure and chose to stop filling my mind with these images that I began feeling spiritually and emotionally healthy again. Instead of feeling depressed over the relationship I wasn't in, I was able to find joy in the life that I had. I even started feeling better about myself when I wasn't constantly comparing myself to the sexy seductresses on television.

This went along way in allowing the Holy Spirit to help me overcome my issues with body image, insecurity, and finding my true identity in Christ. I learned that there truly is freedom in focusing on what is pure and absolutely NOTHING but bondage when you focus on the impure. All of this freedom would not have come without behavior modification.

Then of course, there was the behavior modification that was necessary when we found out about my dad's debt. You see, it wasn't enough to just learn God's financial principles. True freedom from debt and financial bondage came as we consistently began applying these principles to our lives. The truth is that Dave Ramsey's books are great—but they only help you if you follow his advice and do what he says.

Then there were the times that the Holy Spirit called us to change relationships. This one can be tough, but the truth is that many of us have relationships in our lives that are not good for us.

1 Corinthians 15:33 says, **"Do not be misled: 'Bad company corrupts good character.'"**

There were some relationships that we had to end, and others that had to radically change to keep in step with the changes that God was making inside of us.

These are just a few examples of the many ways that the Holy Spirit led me to make lifestyle changes during my time of prayer, Bible reading, and counseling, and the ways I implemented them into my life.

Of course, one of the biggest lifestyle changes that many of us need to implement is scheduling a consistent time of prayer and Bible reading so that the Holy Spirit can speak to us. I mean, it's a nice thing to talk about, but actually doing it requires behavior modification. We have to adjust our schedules; then we have to consistently keep the appointment with Jesus.

No one else can do this for us. It's a commitment that we have to make and keep.

The same thing is true about every behavior or attitude that the Holy Spirit requires you to change. The hard part isn't necessarily hearing his voice or seeing the truth in God's Word, but the obstacle is retraining our human nature, which

Chapter 17 — Lifestyle Changes

doesn't want to change to be obedient and do what is good for it.

Sadly, this is often the step that causes many Christians to detour from the road to healing because they don't want to change. I recently heard a pastor say that one of the most frustrating things for him is when people come into his office wanting their lives to be different but not wanting to make the changes necessary to have a different life.

He said he hears them say, "I'll never go through this situation again."

He thinks, "You will go through it again because you're not willing to change what created the situation in the first place."

However, it doesn't have to be this way. There is another option.

Through the power of the Holy Spirit, you can change.

I can do all this through him who gives me strength (Philippians 4:13).

But thanks be to God! He gives us the victory through our Lord Jesus Christ (I Corinthians 15:57).

Through the power of the Holy Spirit, you can be obedient. You can make the lifestyle changes you need to make. You can be healed and overcome any sin or bondage in your life.

The only thing standing in your way is your decision to do it.

"But you don't get it 'Des, it's not that easy."

Actually, I do get it and I don't think any part of behavior modification is easy. I know there will always be a part of your flesh that doesn't want to change; there will always be

Finding Healing

a part of you that's afraid, that can make an excuse, or that doesn't want to face the pain involved in the change.

I get it because I've been there.

I remember especially when we had to make big changes to our financial lives after the debt was uncovered. I was petrified! I seriously didn't see any way that we could tighten our spending any more; the idea of a budget made me sick, and it seemed like we'd never be able to conquer that mountain. Fortunately, my mom led the charge and we were going to tackle that obstacle no matter how I felt.

And I'm not going to lie to you, it was hard.

There were days that we wanted things we couldn't afford.

There were times when I wondered why God couldn't just perform a miracle and send a check in the mail to pay off the debt and get us back on track.

During this part of the journey, the struggle was real!

Still, we persevered and through the power of the Holy Spirit, we paid off the debt. More importantly, because of the struggle we learned things about ourselves, about God and his Word, and things about how to handle our lives and our finances that we never would have learned

> *Whether or not your heart is healed and you obtain the abundant life Jesus has for you depends on how seriously you obey the Holy Spirit's diagnosis for behavior modification.*

if the problem had been magically solved without lifestyle changes and behavior modifications.

That's one of the reasons that God doesn't usually heal every issue or solve every problem instantly. In the end, his goal isn't necessarily about us always being comfortable—it's about us being made into the men and women that he wants us to be, to be able to do the work he's called us to do in his kingdom.

This can only happen as we submit to the process of change to overcome the obstacles he allows in our lives.

So what is the take away—the big thought from this chapter?

Unfortunately, there is no quick fix or easy five-step process.

All I have is encouragement to be obedient and do what God is telling you to do.

As you pray and read the Bible, go to counseling, and seek to overcome, the Holy Spirit will lead you to make lifestyle changes. When this happens, don't make excuses but JUST DO IT.

Be obedient.

Make the changes.

Avoid the detour and keep doing whatever is necessary to gain your freedom and healing.

As someone who took this very hard road I can tell you that it is 100 percent worth it. Even though I clearly remember days when I would think, "Why does God want me to do this? I'll never be able to do it!" I can look back now and see that everything God required me to give up, change, modify, every friendship I left behind, every new behavior I had to learn was for my good.

They were the changes that brought me healing and gave me the freedom I live in today.

The gain was completely and totally worth all of the pain. I have absolutely no regrets for anytime that I ever said "yes" the Holy Spirit's changes. The truth is that he really does know what is best for us, and even more importantly, he wants us to be healthy, thriving, holy people living the abundant life he has for us.

One of my favorite passages in the Bible is Deuteronomy 30 where Moses is giving his farewell speech to the children of Israel. After going through all of their history and going over God's Laws he says:

> "See, I set before you today life and prosperity, death and destruction. For I command you today to love the Lord your God, to walk in obedience to him, and to keep his commands, decrees and laws; then you will live and increase, and the Lord your God will bless you in the land you are entering to possess.
>
> "But if your heart turns away and you are not obedient, and if you are drawn away to bow down to other gods and worship them, I declare to you this day that you will certainly be destroyed. You will not live long in the land you are crossing the Jordan to enter and possess.
>
> "This day I call the heavens and the earth as witnesses against you that I have set before you life and death, blessings and curses. Now choose life, so that you and your children may live and that you may love the Lord your God, listen to his voice, and hold fast to him. For the Lord is your life, and he will give you many years in the land

he swore to give to your fathers, Abraham, Isaac and Jacob" (Deuteronomy 30:15–21).

Over time, God's ways have not changed.

Today, once again he sets before each of us life and death.

Will we obey or will we detour and continue living in disobedience?

Just as his ways have not changed, his promises and character remain the same.

For those who obey him, he promises life and blessings. Those who disobey suffer the consequences.

Just as he wanted the children of Israel to obey and enter the Promised Land, live in it generation after generation and enjoy it's blessings, so he wants the same for you today.

Still, the choice always rests with us as individuals.

As we said at the beginning, it may be the most challenging choice of all.

God wants to bless you, heal you, set you free, and give you a life that is beyond anything you can imagine.

Now the choice lies with you: Do you want what he has to offer enough to make lifestyle changes?

Chapter 18

Perseverance

> *Therefore, since we are surrounded by such a great cloud of witnesses, let us throw off everything that hinders and the sin that so easily entangles. And let us run with perseverance the race marked out for us, fixing our eyes on Jesus, the pioneer and perfecter of faith. For the joy set before him he endured the cross, scorning its shame, and sat down at the right hand of the throne of God. Consider him who endured such opposition from sinners, so that you will not grow weary and lose heart* (Hebrews 12:3).

$\mathcal{B}$efore we end our time together talking about the road to personal healing and freedom, I'd like to share with you one final word: Perseverance.

The truth is that healing from the pain in our hearts and minds and freedom from the sins and bondages in our lives will not happen overnight.

It takes time . . . it's a process.

There are days during this process when you are going to want to quit.

You're going to get tired, you'll want to give up, and a little voice inside of your head is going to say, *"This isn't worth it."*

I cannot tell you how many times I heard that voice because it was just too many times to count.

Being completely vulnerable, I'll admit that there were lots of times during our years of healing when I just wanted to walk away, figure out how to have a normal life, and abandon God's plan. It wasn't that I didn't love Jesus . . . it was just hard. And it hurt.

It's on those days when you don't feel like continuing on with God's plan that you need *perseverance*—steadfastness in doing something despite difficulty or delay in achieving success.

Basically, you need to stick with it even when you don't want to. When every part of your flesh is screaming, "I want out of this situation NOW," you just keep going.

How do you do it?

First, understand that the desire to quit is normal.

Everyone who has ever gone through the process of healing has wanted to quit at some point along the way. So you're not alone.

Second, take advantage of the rest periods.

During the journey of inner healing, the Holy Spirit will often provide times of rest from the ongoing work of dealing with and overcoming the past. These times are absolute-

> *God's goal isn't about us always being comfortable— it's about us being made into the men and women that he wants us to be.*

ly necessary because they give your heart and your mind a break from the pain and rejuvenate your stamina for the next adventure in healing.

In my life, these "rest periods" usually came in the form of a project in our home. Although it sounds strange, I'll always be grateful that it wasn't just the image of perfect that was falling down in our home during our journey to healing, but our house was also falling apart. Looking back I can see that almost every time we had to face a major secret or issue in our lives, within a few days or weeks, we'd also face a new home repair. Since we were doing the work ourselves, these repairs helped our recovery process. They gave our minds a needed break from the heartache and provided a mental and emotional rest for our souls.

Now obviously, most of you will not have the same type of "rest" (at least you probably hope not!). However, along your journey the Holy Spirit will provide you with your own individual times of rest—a way to breathe fresh air amidst the pain.

Take advantage of these times to rest and refuel. Remember that inner healing is not a sprint, it's a marathon. Along the way you'll need to take time to rest, to recuperate, and be revitalized to tackle the next obstacle.

Just like a boxer takes a few minutes for water, rest, and encouragement from his coach between rounds, we are given "breaks" on our quest for inner healing. Don't despise these times or ignore them. Instead, appreciate and enjoy them for they are the times that refuel your strength to persevere.

Finally, remind yourself that the reward is greater than the pain you're going through right now.

You can only see the finished product God has designed if you keep moving forward and persevering.

Do you not know that in a race all the runners run, but only one gets the prize? Run in such a way as to get the prize. Everyone who competes in the games goes into strict training. They do it to get a crown that will not last, but we do it to get a crown that will last forever. Therefore I do not run like someone running aimlessly; I do not fight like a boxer beating the air. No, I strike a blow to my body and make it my slave so that after I have preached to others, I myself will not be disqualified for the prize (1 Corinthians 9:24–27).

Next, remember, the reward you're fighting to obtain isn't just for today, it's for tomorrow, it's for your children's tomorrow, and ultimately, it will last for eternity.

The truth is that it isn't all about you.

Looking back I can see that the things my mom overcame in her life carried over to my brother and I. All the freedom she fought for, the people she forgave, the counseling she went through, and the generational iniquities she overcame became a platform for my brother and I. It was territory that we didn't have to conquer. We could build on her foundation and overcome our own battles reaching further and further for the kingdom of God.

Today, we carry on her legacy by sharing our testimony. We now use all of the things that we went through, overcame, and experienced healing in to help others see that there is a God who saves, delivers, heals, and makes beautiful things from very imperfect, very ugly situations. Our hope is that as you read our testimony, you will be encouraged to pursue all that God has for your life.

You see, nothing that happens in your life is in vain. God always uses what he does in your life—the healing he gives you, the freedom he provides, all of the things you've learned—so that you can turn around and help someone else through your testimony.

That's why it's important that you persevere—not just for yourself, but because God has a plan to use your healing, your testimony, and your story to show someone else his power to set them free.

Be encouraged that this time will not last forever.

Just like my friend's time of physical therapy came to an end, if you are faithful to follow the Holy Spirit's plan for your life, your time of intense emotional healing will come to an end. Even though the Holy Spirit will continue to work on all of us for the rest of our lives, it isn't always going to be this intense.

Healing will come.

You will walk in freedom.

That's why it's important that you don't give up and quit before you get there.

Let us not become weary in doing good, for at the proper time we will reap a harvest if we do not give up (Galatians 6:9).

As we said at the beginning of the book, there is so much more to life than just surviving—just making it through day after day. God's will is that you have a rich, full, healthy, abundant life.

We pray that you won't just settle for forgiveness of sins and the promise of heaven when you die, but that you'll press forward and persevere.

We hope to whet your appetite to go after all of the healing, freedom, joy, peace, and promises that God has for you.

You see, ultimately, God has a plan for your life. He has a purpose that he wants you to fulfill.

Maybe you can't see it today among all of your pain and heartache, but it's still there.

Standing between you and that promise is your journey to healing.

No, it won't always be easy and yes, there will be days when you want to give up. But don't give in to that temptation. Don't allow yourself to be caught in the knots that want to tangle you back up again.

Keep your eyes on Jesus.

Keep moving forward.

Keep persevering and see this process through to the end.

Do it for all who went before you, do it for yourself, and do it for everyone who will hear your testimony and say, "I want to experience the abundant life they have! I want to pursue the God who can save my soul, heal my heart, restore my future, and fulfill his amazing plan in my life."

I believe in you!

You can do it!

As someone who's been through it and is enjoying the healing on the other side, I can guarantee you'll never regret choosing to follow Jesus on the road to healing. Instead, you'll be amazed just how awesome your life can be as you're living your own **"real and eternal life, more and better life than they ever dreamed of"** (John 10:10, MSG).

Notes

Chapter 7

1. https://www.verywell.com/what-is-shame-425328.

Chapter 8

1. Dave Ramsey, *The Total Money Makeover: A Proven Plan for Financial Fitness.* Nashville, (TN: Thomas Nelson, 2003).

Chapter 10

1. *Disciple's Study Bible: New International Version.* (Nashville, TN: Holman Bible Publishers, 1988), 1348.

Chapter 12

1. http://rickwarren.org/devotional/english/god-wants-us-to-chew-on-his-word.

2. Kenneth L. Barker and John R. Kohlenberger III, *Zondervan NIV Bible Commentary (Volumes I & II).* Grand Rapids, MI: Zondervan Publishing Company, 1994 & 1999.

3. Albert Barnes, *Barnes Notes on the New Testament.* Grand Rapids, MI: Kregel Publications, 1962. Newer print as well as digital editions are available.

4. Albert Barnes, *The New Strong's Expanded Exhaustive Concordance of the Bible.* Nashville, TN: Thomas Nelson, 2010.

We all crave significance. Adessa Holden's book

FINDING SIGNIFICANCE

will help you understand how God sees you, that he loves to speak hope and new life into those that the world sees as insignificant. Each chapter provides questions for reflection, making it a wonderful tool for self or small group study.

Visit **www.adessaholden.com** for details.

Also available in both print and digital formats from Amazon, BarnesandNoble.com, and other online retailers.

About the Author

Adessa Holden is an ordained minister with the Assemblies of God specializing in women's ministry. She's the author of the Finding Healing Curriculum including "Finding Healing", "The Finding Healing Workbook", and the "Finding Healing Video Series." She's also written "Finding Significance" and several e-books.

Whether it be speaking, writing, blogging, or teaching through videos, Adessa's passion is helping women develop an intimate, personal relationship with Jesus and become the women God originally designed them to be.

Adessa is also the Vice-President/Treasurer of 4One Ministries. Together with her brother, Jamie, they travel the East Coast speaking, holding conferences and producing Men's and Women's Resources that provide practical Biblical teaching to strengthen, encourage, and challenge individuals to grow in their walk with Christ and apply Biblical principles to their everyday life.

When asked about herself she'll tell you, "I'm a women's minister, a sister and a daughter. I love to laugh and spend time with people. My favorite things are chocolate, anything purple, summertime (because I can wear sandals), and riding in the car listening to music (which is a good thing since I spend so much time traveling). It is my absolute honor and privilege to serve Jesus and women through this ministry."

Adessa Holden can be contacted at adessa@adessaholden.com, where she welcomes any questions, comments, or requests for speaking engagements.

To read more from Adessa, visit: www.adessaholden.com

www.ingramcontent.com/pod-product-compliance
Lightning Source LLC
LaVergne TN
LVHW051516070426
835507LV00023B/3133